U SING PHONICS TO TEACH READING AND SPELLING

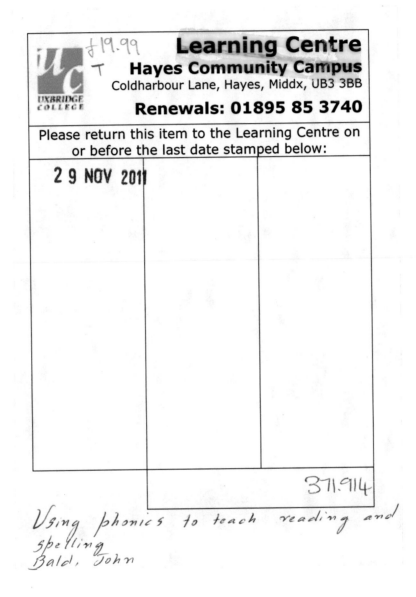

ABOUT THE AUTHOR

John Bald learned to teach in Michael Burton's reading unit at Beaufoy School in Lambeth in the 1970s, and was Tutor in Charge of a Reading and Language Centre in Essex from 1980 to 1993. During this time, he wrote over 100 articles and reviews for the *Times Education Supplement*, and became known as a forthright critic of 'guessing game' theories of reading. He was a consultant on reading to the Dearing review of the national curriculum, a pioneer of training for teaching assistants, and an adviser to the *Who Cares?* Trust on the provision of books for children in care. He is an experienced inspector, and now works as an independant teacher, consultant and journalist. His first book, *The Literacy File*, was joint winner of the United Kingdom Reading Association's Donald Moyle award in 1997. John Bald lives in Linton, Cambridgeshire, with his wife Enid and their Dalmatian, Jasper.

John Bald currently also writes a weblog, which can be found at:

http://johnbald.typepad.com/language

USING PHONICS TO TEACH READING AND SPELLING

John Bald

P·C·P

Paul Chapman
Publishing

Paul Chapman Publishing
A SAGE Publications Company
1 Oliver's Yard
55 City Road
London EC1Y 1SP

SAGE Publications Inc
2455 Teller Road
Thousand Oaks, California 91320

SAGE Publications India Pvt Ltd
B 1/I 1 Mohan Cooperative Industrial Area
Mathura Road, Post Bag 7
New Delhi 110 044

SAGE Publications Asia-Pacific Pte Ltd
33 Pekin Street #02-01
Far East Square
Singapore 048763

Library of Congress Control Number: 2007922696
A catalogue record for this book is available from the British Library

ISBN 978-1-4129-3110-6
ISBN 978-1-4129-3111-3 (pbk)

Typeset by Pantek Arts Ltd, Maidstone, Kent
Printed in Great Britain by Cromwell Ltd, Trowbridge, Wiltshire
Printed on paper from sustainable resources

CONTENTS

CONTENTS OF THE ACCOMPANYING CD

ACKNOWLEDGEMENTS

I am grateful for the support of researchers, authors and publishers who have discussed their work with me and supplied review copies. Particular thanks to Ruth Miskin for allowing me to visit her school on behalf of the *Guardian*, and inviting me to attend her training sessions, and to Maureen Hartley for allowing me to reproduce her Alphabet Songs. Professor Rhona Johnston and Dr Joyce Watson have been generous in sharing and explaining their research, and Jan Turner and Kirsteon Garron of Mapledene Early Years Centre, Hackney, have provided invaluable help with work with under-fives. Thanks also to Keith Duggan, Louisa Lochner and Julie Brown for sharing their thoughts and practical ideas. Any errors are, of course, entirely my responsibility.

The book would not have been written without the confidence and encouragement of my wife Enid Smith, who has also provided essential guidance on scientific method and developments in brain research.

John Bald

This is a book about using phonics to teach reading and spelling to children and adults. It is not an evangelical tract, and does not pretend that phonics are all that we need. English spelling is not an exact match for English speech, and therefore phonics do not always work. Therefore, while I agree with Jim Rose (2006: 4) that

> *The systematic approach, which is generally understood as 'synthetic' phonics, offers the vast majority of young children the best and most direct route to becoming skilled readers and writers,*

I also believe that he has failed to tackle the key problem of explaining irregularity and helping learners, children and adults, to handle it. Evidence from brain scanning shows that the brain adapts its structures to deal with the demands of different languages. In English, the brain adapts itself to interpret the information conveyed by letters as we read and spell. The structures and techniques in this book promote this process of adaptation and interpretation as well as teaching phonics. Nevertheless, the basic phonic structure of the language remains central to learning to read and write. We use other sources of information in addition to phonics, and not instead of phonics.

Each chapter is self-contained, with suggestions for further reading. Names and identities in all case studies have been changed to ensure anonymity of the children concerned. The accompanying CD contains a selection of supporting activities that I have found particularly useful. It does not, however, set out to duplicate or compete with the games recommended in Chapter 7. There is an Appendix of key patterns in English spelling, including irregular patterns, and a Glossary.

I welcome correspondence from readers, who may contact me by e-mail at johnbald@talktalk.net.

FOREWORD

John Bald has been a significant figure in the literacy education field for many years. His articles, letters and conference presentations have provided a distinctive contribution to some long-standing debates, particularly on the role of phonics in literacy development.

In this book he brings together his experience as teacher, course provider and school inspector to offer guidance on using phonics to teach reading and spelling. While there has been an increase in the number of publications on this topic in recent years, it is important to recognise that John Bald has argued for phonic methods for many years, including during a time when their importance was not as widely recognised as it is today.

The book also reflects John's use of research findings to illuminate his thinking – he was the first to alert me to the publication of Marilyn Jager Adams' seminal work *Beginning to Read* – and his book's guidance is interspersed with references to authorities who have influenced him. He goes to some lengths to show why these sources are important, for our broader understanding of language and the English writing system, as well as for the teaching of reading and phonics.

But John's book is primarily a practical one, with the liberal use of activites, child case studies and anecdotal asides. Throughout, John's concerns are to interest his audience, as well as to advise them, so that the work that they do with children is underpinned with an appreciation of the 'why', as well as the 'how', and that this work reflects the many purposes and pleasures in using written language.

Roger Beard
Professor of Primary Education
Institute of Education
University of London

CHAPTER 1

Phonics, Why and How

This chapter will:

■ Explain why phonics are important in teaching reading and writing

■ Outline complex phonic patterns, and the roots of irregularity

■ Explain the principles of teaching phonics

■ Introduce and define key terms, including synthetic and analytic phonics

■ Consider some alternative theories of reading

Phonics is the systematic teaching of the sounds conveyed by letters and groups of letters, and includes teaching children to combine and blend these to read or write words. It is of crucial importance, for the following reasons:

■ The majority of the information conveyed by letters concerns sounds.

■ Letters tell us more than any other source of information, even when we have to interpret the information they provide.

■ We cannot read fluently until we read accurately, and this depends on accurate use of the information conveyed by letters. Skilled, fluent readers very rarely guess.

■ Once we have learned what the letters are telling us in a word, we can store it in our memory and retrieve it more quickly than if we had to work it out.

■ As English is not completely regular, most children are unlikely to be able to perceive and use patterns in language for themselves (Rose 2006: 18).

■ Direct observation (Rose 2006: 66–9) in schools has shown a consistent link between phonics and successful reading.

■ Almost all weak readers have difficulty in blending sounds from
letters to make words. Almost all good readers do this well.

Regular and irregular languages

Alphabetic writing represents the sounds we hear in words by means of letters.
For reading, learners reconstruct the word by blending the sounds represented by
the letters. For spelling, they translate the sounds in words into letters. Although
letters often give us more than sounds, their links with sounds are their most
consistent and important feature, and there is some link with sound in every
word. Children and adults who can use this connection fluently and accurately
build up a store of words that they can read very quickly. Familiar words are
scanned swiftly, as they contain information that has already been learned and
stored in the memory, while learners have a valuable technique for working out
new words, even when the sound connection does not tell the whole story.

In some languages, notably Spanish, Finnish and Italian, the links between
sounds and letters are very consistent – what you see is what you say. In
English, the connections between sounds and letters have been affected by historical events and long-term changes in speech and pronunciation. As a result,
phonics work most, but not all of the time, and we have to adapt our brain to
interpret what letters tell us rather than simply translate letters into sounds and
vice versa. This means that we need to take care in presenting phonics, so that
children do not become confused when they come across words in which the
letters do not behave as expected. The main causes of irregularity in English are:

■ In the 150 years after the Norman conquest of 1066, English was
flooded with French. The spelling of roughly one-third of
English words reflects this – *table*, for example, makes perfect
phonic sense in French, where *l* is pronounced before *e*. Try it.

■ Over the centuries since English began to be written down,
several letters which used to be pronounced, such as *k* in *knight*,
no longer are. They are still retained in spelling. Modern,
everyday speech takes further shortcuts, particularly at the ends
of words and in pronouncing vowel (voice) sounds.

■ In the late Middle Ages, there was a shift in the way vowels were
pronounced. Some words are spelled as they were before the

shift, and so vowel sounds are not always written as we now speak them. The most common example is probably *was*.

What is a Vowel?

Most of us have been taught that vowels are the five letters, *a*, *e*, *i*, *o* and *u*. But a vowel is first and foremost a sound made with the voice, and the letters we know as vowels have the difficult task of catching and representing these voice sounds. The system of voice sounds in English is complicated. It includes composite vowels, known as *diphthongs*, which begin in one part of the mouth and move to another — say *boy*, and feel how your tongue moves upwards as you pronounce the *oy*.

Knowing when and when not to pronounce a letter, how to pronounce it, and what emphasis to give different parts of similar words (*photograph, photographic, photography*) requires us to interpret what the letters tell us in the context of what we know about the word's meaning. *The Learning Brain*, by Sarah-Jayne Blakemore and Uta Frith, FRS (2005), summarises key evidence from brain scans that show readers in English using a distinct section of the brain, between the processing areas and long-term memory storage, that is concerned with interpreting information from letters after it has been processed. This area was not active in Italian readers, whose language is regular, but was very active in English readers. This shows that the brain adapts itself in different ways to the demands of different languages.

Letter combinations

Early in the disputes over phonics in the National Curriculum, the Conservative minister Kenneth Clarke, asked what he meant by phonics, replied 'c-a-t says cat'. So it does, provided we take care not to add stray bits of vowel to the *c* and *t*, producing an effect like *ke a te*. But three-letter words such as *cat* make up a small minority of English, as scanning a few lines of almost any text will show. Many words use letters in combinations, and these do not always reflect what we might expect the letters to produce on their own. Some writers on phonics refer to a two-letter combination as a *digraph*, and a three-letter combination as a *trigraph*. In my experience, children are happy with the term *group*, and so am I.

A group in which letters do as we might expect is *sh*. Words like *ship* or *finish* show fairly clearly elements of both letters in the group, and this one is easy to learn. Words such as *patient, station*, though, use the group *ti* to produce the same sound as *sh*, and this is far removed from the normal sound produced by *ti*, as in *tip*. This type of group requires a greater adjustment of thinking in order to learn and use it. Similarly, the softening effect of *e, i* and *y* after c – *face, city, bicycle* – and, most of the time after *g* – *generous, ginger, Egypt* – requires us to modify our first choice of sound for *c* and *g*, and to use a system of alternative letters (*kettle, kill, Kylie*) or blocking letters (*plague, guilty*) if we want to keep the sound of these letters hard.

The most frequent combination of letters, and one that demands an early adjustment of thinking, is final *e* that alters the sound at the end of a three-letter word such as *mad* to *made* (or *here, bite, note* and *cute*). Children often find it harder to discriminate between vowels than consonants in the first place, and this additional demand requires a further, major adjustment to their thinking.

Some current writers refer to *e* in these words as a *split digraph*, teaching it with other two-letter vowel groups; this is also an effective way to present the pattern. Each English vowel letter represents more than one sound, and, most of the time, this is indicated by grouping it with another letter. Common vowel groups are *ai, ay, au, aw, ee, ea, ei, oo, ou, oi, oy* (*raid, stay, autumn, awful, steep, tea, eight, stool, out, boil, boy*). Adding an *e* after the vowel can be seen as making a group, or digraph, *ae, ee, ie, oe, ue*, which may be split by another letter (*hate, complete, site, vote, lute*).

There is no clear evidence as to whether the split group approach or the concept of having one letter change the sound of another is better – it is a matter of professional judgement, and may depend on the age of the learners and how much they already know. It is beyond doubt, though, that in learning to read and spell in English we have to do much more than put single letters together to make words – we have also to learn, understand and interpret the use of letters in combinations and groups.

How do we tackle irregularity and letter combinations in teaching?

We need, above all, to be careful in what we say, so that we do not lead learners to think that the language is more regular than it really is. It is important to take care not to use absolute statements, unless we are completely sure that they are right. If we use, from the beginning, phrases such as 'usually', 'most of the time' or 'nearly always', we help children build up the idea that phonics are likely to help, but do not give any false guarantees. The importance of these qualifying statements is often greatest when children are reading on their own or at home, where the teacher is not on hand to provide prompts. Learners can't know in advance whether a word is regular or not, or even when letters are used in combinations, and they need to be prepared for the times when phonics don't work. The case study below shows what can happen if a child learns nothing more than applying one sound to each word.

CASE STUDY

Paul, 7

Paul came to see me because of a serious problem with reading, for which he had already had over a year of private lessons. Paul knew most of the sounds conveyed by letters, but tried to read by calling out the sound of each letter and then guessing at the word. When he came to *the*, he tried several times to make the sounds *t – h – e* into a recognisable word, became frustrated, and settled for *ten*. Paul's understanding of phonics as a single sound for each letter was preventing him from learning to read, and effective teaching began with helping him to adjust his thinking to take account of combinations and to blend rather than sounding out one letter at a time. By the end of our first lesson, Paul had read the cover and page one of *The Cat in the Hat*.

When I was learning to drive, my instructor told me 'we believe everything the mirror tells us, but we don't believe the mirror tells us everything.' For a long time, I used this in teaching reading, substituting *letters* for *mirror*. This was helpful, but it became increasingly clear that we couldn't always believe everything the letters told us – silent *p* at the beginning of words didn't really tell us anything. So, the maxim I teach is now:

We use what the letters tell us, but we don't believe the letters tell us everything.

This is consistent with experience of everyday life, from an early age into adulthood. Are children good all of the time, or most of the time? Is Mummy (or their teacher!) in a good mood all, or most of the time? Can we rely on the train all of the time, most of the time, or some of the time? We all have our mental picture of what we can and cannot rely on, and of the conditions that make things more, or less, reliable. We build up a similar mental picture as we learn to read, and part of our task as teachers is to help learners to do this.

Synthetic phonics: the mainspring

When we read, we retrieve and put together information that has been set down using the alphabetic system, and when we write, we use it to represent, in order, the sounds that we would otherwise say. This is *synthetic phonics*, or *word-building*. Teaching schemes based on synthetic phonics have these points in common:

- Letter–sound correspondences are taught in a clearly defined sequence.

- Children have a short, pacy lesson each day.

- The initial programme typically takes a little over a term to complete.

- Children are taught how to blend sounds to make words, and practise this.

- They learn to spell at the same time as they learn to read.

- Teaching uses attractive resources, songs, games and actions.

- Teaching provides many opportunities for language development.

The most important point is that they require children to blend sounds from letters to read words, and the next most important point is that they do this in a systematic way, beginning with the most straightforward combinations of vowel–consonant–vowel words, and gradually introducing more complex patterns. This approach has the long-term benefit of preparing children for advanced reading, when they will meet regular letter combinations in prefixes and suffixes.

Synthetic phonics enables readers to extract and use the information represented by letters, and, with practice, to build up a store of words that are read so quickly that they seem to take almost no time to work out. Teachers sometimes refer to these as 'sight vocabulary' or just 'words recognised at sight', though the most sophisticated tracking systems (Bald 2003) have provided evidence that we are, in effect, tracking the contours of the letters with our eyes in order to distinguish one from another. This process is so fast that words are fed into our mind virtually instantaneously, and we are then able to group them together into meaningful phrases.

Synthetic phonics in spelling is easily integrated with reading. Children can build words using plastic or magnetic letters as they learn to read them. This avoids them having to write each word by hand in the early stages, allowing all their attention to be focused on the sounds and letters so that they have maximum opportunity to understand and reinforce the connections. The action research in Clackmannanshire (Johnston and Watson 2005) was particularly successful in promoting spelling.

The emphasis on the language-rich curriculum, initially through games, songs and stories, is important. Some children have very limited experience of language outside school, and are totally dependent on their school or nursery both to teach the basic skills of using language for communication and to liberate their imaginations. Rose's (2006) recommendation that phonics lessons should be 'discrete' means that teaching needs to be specific and systematic, but not that phonics should be taught in isolation from everything else – on the contrary, children should be encouraged to see patterns and apply sounds and sound patterns in a wide range of activities, including nursery rhymes, poems, puppetry, telling and retelling stories.

CASE STUDY

Tommy and 'Arabella Miller'

When Tommy joined the nursery in an Essex port town, he communicated by pointing and making sounds, with an occasional single word. Tommy enjoyed rhymes, particularly 'Arabella Miller':

Little Arabella Miller

Had a furry caterpillar.

First it sat upon her mother

Then upon her baby brother.

▶

They said, 'Naughty Arabella Miller,

Take away that caterpillar.'

Tommy would sit in the front row at assembly and joyfully belt out this rhyme, with its three sentences and twenty-seven words. It was not just an exercise in sound patterns, but a framework for extending language and participation in a shared activity.

Synthetic phonics schemes: two controversial points

- Irregular words are taught separately, but irregularity is not explained.

- Books are not introduced until children have learned to read the most common regular words.

Current phonics schemes teach irregular words as 'sight words', but neither they nor Rose explain why some words are irregular, and why, therefore, phonics do not always work. This issue is tackled in Chapter 4.

The slight delay in introducing books in phonics lessons has been criticised, but need not cause problems if the language-rich curriculum is properly understood. Modern phonic schemes are accompanied by stories, rhymes, short texts and other language activities. There is no evidence of negative attitudes resulting from this work. If, though, schools choose to use books from the beginning, it is important that they explain clearly to children that not all words work as we expect, so that they do not become confused when they meet an irregular word.

Analytic phonics: a subordinate tool

Analytic phonics is *wordbreaking*. Children are presented with words and learn to pick out letters and to associate them with the sounds they represent. In some schools, analytic phonics has been used as an alternative to synthetic phonics in initial reading teaching, and is sometimes reduced to having children identify the first letter in a word. The approach does not teach children to blend sounds to make words. Analytic phonics is not, therefore, an effective vehicle for initial reading teaching.

But we know that synthetic phonics does not always work, and it is at this point that analytic phonics is needed. For example, in the words *know, knight, knuckle,* and *write, wrong, wrap,* analysis shows us that the initial, silent letter, is always followed by the same letter. This is so regular that the two letters can be considered as a little phonic group, much like *qu.* Used in this way, analytic phonics enables children to learn substantial groups of words, many of them very common, that require an adjustment to our normal interpretation of letter sounds. Compare *warm, water, war,* for example, with *bat, sat, that.*

The influence of analysis in these examples is so clear that analytic phonics simply cannot be excluded from the teaching of reading in English. Its place, though, is subordinate to that of synthetic phonics. Even after we have analysed irregular patterns, we need to blend them with the regular ones in order to read the words.

Alternatives to phonics

Alternatives to phonics as a basis for reading and spelling have been proposed since the middle of the nineteenth century. Early theories were based on objections to boring, drill-based teaching. They proposed teaching whole words, leading to an approach known as 'look and say' that became widespread in the middle of the last century. Later theories attempted to combine evidence from psychology and linguistics – hence the term *psycholinguistics,* whose chief advocates are the writers Kenneth Goodman (1978) and Frank Smith (1967). The latest alternative theory was the Department for Education and Skills's (DfES) Searchlights (DfES 1998), in which phonics, grammatical knowledge, the reader's previous knowledge, and context were all held to work together to shed light on words.

This is not the place to discuss all of these theories in detail, but the following are among their most significant flaws:

■ Whole-word reading does not give children the information they need to work words out for themselves, leaving those who do not learn to do this for themselves to fail

■ Kenneth Goodman's theory (for example, 1967), that readers predict what is going to come next and then check their predictions by sampling the text, has been disproved by direct observation of readers in action.

- Goodman's miscue analysis, still widely used for assessment, relies solely on a reader's errors for information about his or her thinking, and does not take account of what is read correctly.

- Frank Smith's assertion that English spelling is too irregular to be used as a basis for reading is based on the application of strict logic to the system. The mathematical theory of 'fuzzy logic', in which members of a set have most, but not all of its characteristics, is a more accurate fit for English spelling, and allows computers to read text aloud, a procedure Smith (1978: 51) held to be impossible because spelling was so irregular.

- Searchlights' single model of reading did not take account of changes in readers' needs as their store of known words and vocabulary develops, and appeared to give phonics equal status with other sources of information at all stages. It had no basis in research (Schatz and Baldwin 1986).

Rose's main recommendations and their implications

This is a summary of Rose's (2006: 70–72) main recommendations followed by a comment on their implications.

- High-quality, systematic phonic work as defined by the review should be taught discretely. The knowledge, skills and understanding that constitute high-quality phonic work should be taught as the prime approach in learning to decode (to read) and encode (to write/spell) print.

Phonics teaching needs to be systematic. The term 'discretely' implies that the work needs to be covered in specific lessons, and not simply as it arises in the course of other literacy activities. The term 'prime' means that phonic work should be the main approach to reading and spelling.

- Phonic work should be set within a broad and rich language curriculum that takes full account of developing the four interdependent strands of language: speaking, listening, reading and writing, and enlarging children's stock of words.

Schools need to plan for language development in all of the activities children undertake, and to ensure that teachers and assistants understand the ways in which language strands depend on and contribute to each other. Reading, for example, extends children's knowledge of words and sentence structures beyond those most will meet in everyday conversation outside school, and this contributes to writing. Our knowledge, understanding and confidence with words is built up by successful use of them in speaking as well as in writing.

- For most children, high-quality, systematic phonic work should start by the age of five. This should be preceded by pre-reading activities that pave the way for such work to start.

This implies that teachers will have to track young children's progress in language and early literacy activities carefully, in order to make sure that they are introduced to phonic work as soon as they are ready for it, but not before. There will be a need to intensify support for children who are not making normal progress.

- Phonic work for young children should be multi-sensory in order to capture their interest, sustain motivation, and reinforce learning in imaginative and exciting ways.

Multi-sensory work may be on a large scale, such as puppet shows, or on a smaller scale, such as manipulating plastic letters or playing phonic games on the computer.

- The Early Years Foundation Stage and the renewed literacy framework must be compatible with each other and make sure that expectations about continuity and progression in phonic work are expressed explicitly in the new guidance.

These materials are available from www.dfes.gov.uk.

- Additional support must be compatible with mainstream practice. Irrespective of whether intervention work is taught in regular lessons or elsewhere, the gains made by children through such work must be sustained and built upon when they return to their mainstream class.

Support and class teachers need to plan together so that additional teaching builds on and reinforces the work children do in class. The progress of children receiving additional teaching needs to be tracked particularly closely for this purpose.

■ Phonic work needs to be managed, monitored and supported by feedback and training. It should inform governors' target-setting. One member of staff needs to be fully able to lead on literacy, especially phonic work.

This recommendation builds on the enhanced role of language co-ordinators developed during the National Literacy Strategy. Part of the work will include keeping up to date with revisions in national guidance, and adapting them to the specific needs of the school.

Pause for reflection ...

What in your own teaching of reading and spelling do you find works best, and what causes you the most difficulty?

How do you explain to children why letters don't always behave as we expect?

Which of Rose's recommendations will have most impact on your school?

FURTHER READING

Independent Review of the Teaching of Reading. Jim Rose (2006) London: DfES. Rose's review has been extensively misrepresented. He is entitled to be judged on the basis of what he says, and not on what other people say that he says. The review can be found on www.dfes.gov.uk.

The Roots of Phonics: A Historical Introduction, Miriam Balmuth (1982) New York: McGraw-Hill. A comprehensive survey of the roots of sound–letter correspondences in English, and of the ways in which these have been handled in teaching. A particularly valuable book for students, as it brings together a wealth of material that is not readily available elsewhere. It has useful discussion of the early history of alternatives to phonics.

Key Elements in Synthetic Phonics

This chapter will:

- Help plan the transition from early language development to phonic work
- Consider schemes of work, planning and teaching lessons
- Help you get the best from teaching assistants
- Provide an outline of recording work and tracking progress
- Consider additional assessment for children with learning difficulties

---

Modern settings for children under five are well organised to promote social and intellectual development. These goals are closely intertwined with language development. Settings are laid out with a range of interesting and stimulating activities so that, whatever children choose to do, they will be doing something the teacher would like them to do. In effect, much of the teaching is built into the environment, so that there is a productive triangle between the activity, the child and the adults. This arrangement provides an equally effective focal point for social interaction, which in turn promotes the development of spoken language beyond that which children need to meet their own immediate needs. As they are not constantly directing activities, adults are free to observe the children, to identify needs and track progress. At the same time, children will be learning to listen to and retell stories and rhymes, often being asked explicitly what they think, which parts they like best.

All of these features put early years practitioners in a strong position to decide when a child is ready to begin phonic work. The key questions are *Will the child benefit from the teaching?* and *Will the child understand it?* The lists below provide sources of evidence that will help with the decision. The record sheet (supplied on the accompanying CD) can be used to collate this evidence, at the same time providing a simple screening mechanism to identify children who need extra help.

Children making good progress in early language development

- Take an active part in conversations with adults and other children.

- Begin to speak in phrases or sentences rather than single words.

- Enjoy stories, understand them, keep focused and can sometimes retell them.

- Join in nursery rhymes, beginning to remember them.

- Pick up books and look at them, spontaneously or with prompting.

- Notice words and letters in names, captions, asking questions about them.

- Imitate letters in drawing and play; controlling brush or pencil.

- Have favourite stories or rhymes, and ask for them.

Additional activities for slower starters

- Sharing books intensively.

- Planned individual activities involving stories.

- Work with puppets and soft toys of characters from stories.

- Adding actions and movements to stories to maintain engagement.

- Focused conversation with adults, based on the child's observed interests.

- Digital photos of child's interests and environment as focal point for conversation .

- Activities designed to promote these interests, for example, an interest in animals.

- Extra activities involving letters, for example captioning, artwork, making name with plastic letters, decorating names and drawing attention to letters.

- Matching, selecting and naming activities from the Portsmouth Down's Syndrome Project (now the Down's Education Trust, www.downsed.org).

Language development record

Add additional + signs to indicate strengths, and – signs to indicate concerns.

Language development record. Class:

Name	Conversation	Sentences	Stories	Rhyme	Interest in books	Noticing letters	Date started phonics

Sharing books intensively

The case study below shows how a careful introduction to books can develop much more than reading skills.

CASE STUDY

Cushla and her books

Cushla was born in New Zealand, and had a wide range of learning and emotional difficulties. In the first months of her life, she was in such distress that she screamed and wailed day and night. Her mother began to place Dick Bruna books in front of her face and tell her stories based on them. Dick Bruna's books have simple pictures, with strong lines and primary colours. Cushla learned to focus her eyes on these pictures, and this became the starting point for her relationship with her parents, the development of language, and an abiding interest in books and stories. At one point, on measures of awareness of books, Cushla's scores were above average, leading some people to question whether it was possible to knock out her handicaps completely. Once she started school, however, Cushla reached a plateau at about the 7-year-old level. The experience had enriched her life, and that of her parents, and had maximised progress. Her grandmother, Dorothy Butler, ran a children's bookshop, and recorded the process in her classic book (Butler 1979).

These are the key points we can learn from Cushla's experience:

- Match the book to the child's needs and interests.

- Not everything will work, so you need a good selection.

- Make time to go over the child's favourites as often as he or she wants.

- Give the child as much choice as possible, and follow that choice.

- Children need their own books as well as library or school books.

- Early progress does not mean that we have solved all of a child's problems.

Planned individual activities involving stories

The nursery at Great Harwood Primary School, Blackburn, has a series of activities to engage parents in conversation with their children. Book and story bags include costumes of the characters, so that children can dress up and act out the stories with their parents. A favourite is *Handa's Surprise* (Brown 1995), in which a monkey steals fruit from a basket. It comes with a straw hat, plastic fruit with Velcro, a sari, monkey's ears and tail. The bag for *Princess Bear* (Stewart 2001) contains a princess outfit, with jewellery box, beads – useful for counting – and lacey bits. (This is surprisingly popular with boys.) The varied contents of the bags have encouraged parents to use more books, and children ask to take them home.

Stuart, an older child at Great Harwood, had missed out on early play, and was sent to 'help' in the nursery each afternoon. He gained confidence both from playing in the nursery and from the idea that he was helping the adults. A favourite activity was a type of jigsaw with a baseboard, into which he fitted animals and objects. An adult working with Stuart would help him by asking Stuart to pass objects for him to put into the jigsaw. Selecting the named objects enabled Stuart to make connections between them and words. After a little time, Stuart would use the jigsaws he had learned from with the other children, using the language he had learned from the adult to help them. The activity contributed much to his personal development, as well as helping him to develop both vocabulary and tactful communication with other children. 'It might have red on it …', 'It might be over here …'.

CASE STUDY

Animal models and early language

Sally joined Great Harwood nursery unable to speak. The nursery made a regular feature of animals at work, and used tables set up with models to promote talk. Sally's teachers began with the noises a lion and a monkey would make. Sally learned to imitate these noises, and to associate different noises with different animals. This was the beginning of control over the sounds she was making. Over time, teachers and carers moved from models to animations from the Internet. Sally came to recognise more animals and to make a broader range of sounds. She found that other children began to recognise the sounds she was making, and would imitate them. This gave her a sense of achievement, and carers joined in, taking Sally to the zoo. The process allowed carers to see improvement in Sally's language, and helped allay their fears for her ability to adapt to school life. The support teachers developed this into using animal puppets to extend language, and Sally gradually moved from saying only one word at a time to combining words, such as *lion — roar*.

Puppets, soft toys and characters from stories

When a class started a new book, Gill Banks, headteacher of Nabbotts Infant School in Essex, would invite parents to make a soft toy of the main character. These were of high quality, and brought to life stories such as *Mrs Honey's Hat* (Adams 1998) in which birds steal fruit from her hat as she goes to church, *The Very Hungry Caterpillar* (Carle 2002) and *Penguin Small* (Inkpen 2006). For the *Lighthouse Keeper's Lunch* (Armitage and Armitage 1994), the staff made most of the classroom into a display that children used to act out the stories.

Acting out and retelling stories

Acting out and retelling stories helps children to extend their use of language by limiting the demands made on them – the story is already written, and they contribute their own interpretation. Californian storyteller Priscilla Maynard adds props, including a baseboard map of the story, characters on laminated sheets and simple costumes, which provide a further series of aids and prompts to children who find it difficult to remember events in sequence. She found that the props enabled young children to produce a fuller version of *The Three Billy Goats Gruff* than they could without them. The approach can be extended to any learning activity that has a story element, such as religious or historical stories, and remains valuable throughout the infant school.

Matching, selecting, naming

Peter's parents brought him to me early in 2005 because he was unable to read from his school's reading scheme, which was not based on phonics. Peter was five, and had significant difficulties with speech and language. He had been receiving help from a major teaching hospital since early childhood, and had extensive and warm support from his parents and older sister. I had previously used techniques from the Portsmouth Down's Syndrome project to help weak readers, and had found them easy to adapt to individual needs. I used them in conjunction with other techniques for weak readers, as set out in Chapter 8.

I first explained to Peter that letters usually told us about the sounds that made up words, and demonstrated this with simple, three-letter words. As weak readers usually find it easier to recognise patterns at the ends of words rather than the beginning, I began with *sun*, and altered the initial letter to *fun, run, gun* and so on, using plastic letters. We took this very slowly at first, and I modelled sounding and blending the letters carefully. Mixing up the plastic letters and having Peter make words made a good game, and he enjoyed getting them right. We took our time, until he could make all of the words confidently.

We then moved to his reading scheme book. Peter and his family wanted to keep with this if at all possible, and the school did not have any alternative. I explained to Peter that sometimes letters did not tell us all we needed to know in order to read a word, and that sometimes the same letter told us different things. We then started on the first page of the book, and I explained the patterns in the irregular words as we went along. Peter understood the explanations, but found it hard to remember the words once we moved on.

Professor Sue Buckley's Portsmouth scheme involves first matching, then selecting, then naming, pictures and words. The matching stage is essential for most children with Down's Syndrome, but other learners rarely need it. The selecting stage, in which children hand the teacher a card or a slip of paper with a word the teacher asks for, is a very useful half-way house in helping children to learn and remember words, as the child has only to link the sounds with the letters as he hears them, rather than reproduce the sounds for himself. Peter was hesitant at first and made some mistakes – when this happens, you just put the word the child offers back, and ask again, reinforcing the right answer with the right measure of praise. After a few minutes, Peter was able to hand me all the words as I called them out, and could name most of them for himself. (For the naming stage, I let Peter pick the order at first.)

The session had taken 45 minutes, a long time for Peter. Would he be able to remember the words next week? He came straight in, sat down while I was still greeting his parents, and started to read. We moved quickly through the rest of the book. Whenever he got stuck, I would explain the phonic pattern and any variation behind the word, and would then teach it by moving to another word with the same pattern. (For example, I would teach *mother* by working on *brother* and *other*, coming back to *mother* once these words were secure.) Where necessary, I would put more words on slips of paper and have Peter select them, but we needed to do this less often, and his recognition speed improved rapidly. The following week, he had changed his book and was making rapid, confident progress. Reading quickly became a strength. The work was reinforced by a sympathetic speech therapist working with Peter at school, and contributed to his discharge from the teaching hospital's clinic.

Note: Readers in Northern Ireland, Wales and Scotland should note that the recommendations in this chapter are based on current provision in England, and may need to be adjusted in the light of their own national requirements.

Pause for reflection ...

How does your nursery or reception class plan for the language development of children who are making less than normal progress? Which aspects of this work are most successful, and is there any pattern to them? Are there any areas that need further development? If so, is there any pattern in these?

What resources do you use, and how effective are they? In particular, do you have a good range of books to involve all the children, with additional activities surrounding the books?

What systems do you have to work with these children's parents, and how do the parents view them?

How do you record progress?

Scheme of work: write or buy?

A scheme of work should be a practical, working document that helps teachers and assistants plan teaching and learning, and track progress. It should also be flexible enough to be altered to take account of day-to-day information from assessment, so that assessment contributes to learning. Most schools adopting a phonic approach use one of the main schemes as a core; these are discussed in

Chapter 7. All have an inbuilt scheme of work. In *Fast Phonics First*, for example, the scheme of work is built into the software, and complete lesson plans are included in the handbook. There is similar detail in the other main core schemes. You may well, therefore, find that the published scheme meets your needs with little or no alteration. If so, do not write another – Rose (2006) notes that many successful schools have adopted this approach. You can still keep the core scheme under review, and with notes on what works best and what modifications you might need to make in practice. If, in time, these notes amount to a new scheme of work, then that is the time to write one, preferably using information and communication technology (ICT).

Good reasons for writing your own scheme might include having a significant number of children with serious learning difficulties whose work you wish to integrate with that of the rest of the class, or good systems for explaining some aspects of phonics that are not in the scheme. A school's own scheme may help new teachers and assistants to adapt to its approach, quickly. This means it has to be easy to read and to use. To allow continuous evaluation and revision, it is best to set up a simple format on the computer, and add rows/columns as needed. An outline format is included on the accompanying CD and reproduced below.

Scheme of work key features checklist

- A clearly thought-out sequence of activities
- Notional timings
- Clearly specified, linked resources with a note on their use
- A *What next?* column with extension materials for higher-attaining children
- An *Extra help* column with notes on reinforcement work for slower learners
- An evaluation column

Scheme of work format

Note: To expand this outline, click *Table* then *Add rows*. Rows will expand automatically as you type. The sample rows are for reference only. You may choose landscape or portrait format.

Try this:

You can save a lot of time when typing by setting up shortcuts in Word, as follows:

Highlight the word or phrase, e.g. special educational needs.
In the top bar, click *Tools*, then *Autocorrect*.
The highlighted word or phrase appears in a box. Add your shortcut (e.g. sn – not sen, as you might want to use that as an abbreviation).
Click *OK*.
Next time you type sn, Word will insert the complete phrase.
Use with any word you type frequently, and the amount of keying you do can be cut by up to two-thirds.

Term 1

Letter pattern	Timing	Activities and resources	What next?	Extra help	Evaluation
Short vowel, a	30 min.	CVC words a – wide variety. Introduce, demonstrate blending with song. Children wear letter tabards, move around to make words. Make their own words with magnetic letters. Write one word without copying and illustrate it. Sing song to recap.	Find, read and understand longer words with short a sound – *caravan, catamaran, catapult*, etc. See how many words they can write without looking.	TA session p.m. Magnetic letters. Word building cards/ dominoes. Nessy game. Song.	
Short vowel, e	30 min.	As above, but with final session revising a as well as e.	Longer words as above, e.g. *elephant*.	As above.	
etc.					

Sample entry from Year 2 scheme of work

Soft c and g: introduction

Activity	Timing	Resources	What next?	Extra help	Evaluation
Whole class session, demonstrating softening effects of *e, i, y* on *c* and *g*. Explaining that it doesn't always work with *g* (*get, girl, gear*) because of historical factors. – e.g 'gurle' as an an of *girl*. Group work practising reading words with these features, using games made from word lists.	30 min. + 20 min. group work	Whiteboard + Clicker 5® Word-lists. Blank playing cards, marked up with *ce, ci, cy, ge, gi, gy*. **Games:** Bingo Snap Snakes and ladders. Pelmanism	Find at least 3 (or 5 if appropriate) words with each combination at the beginning, middle and ends of words.	Individual help with assistant or teacher in selecting work and then forming words with cards or using Clicker 5®. Extra individual practice using the games.	

The scheme of work format provides an outline of activities for a lesson, but does not contain a complete lesson plan – this is for the individual teacher to make, on the basis of the progress made by his or her class, and the kind of presentation they find most effective. It may be convenient to print off the scheme in landscape format, and to make notes on this hard copy. The most important discipline is to fill in the evaluation section consistently, so that co-ordinators can use it to keep track of what is and is not working. In turn, checking these needs to be a regular part of each co-ordinator's work.

What makes an effective lesson?

Teachers and children know instinctively when they have had a successful lesson, and successful phonics lessons have much in common with those in other fields. However, the content of a phonics lesson can be dry, and much depends on giving each child a sense that they understand what they are doing, and are making progress. This is particularly important for those who are making average and below-average progress. Most successful learners know that they are doing well because the correct answers they supply ensure a steady supply of praise, from parents and family as well as from teachers. Weaker learners know that they are not getting everything right and need more rein-forcement, both to their self-confidence and to their learning. The following are key points for successful phonics lessons.

- **The material is matched to what children need to learn**: This requires accurate assessment of what they already know, and clear understanding of what they need to learn next. A well organised scheme of work helps, but needs to be used in conjunction with your professional judgement, as much for the most able as for the weakest learners. If children catch on to something quickly, you need to have the flexibility to build on it and move on, otherwise they will become bored. If they find something difficult, you need to have several angles to approach it from – often a good variety of games.

- **You and the children know what they have learned**: As we read, information comes from the page to our eyes at the speed of light, and is processed by our brain using electrochemical links that can operate almost as quickly. To use the process effectively and hence read fluently, we need to be able to read words without working them out each time. Therefore, as well as mastering new material, learning in phonics lessons often takes the form of speeding up what is already known, so that word recognition becomes virtually automatic. Once again, you need to be aware of the full range of learning that is going on in the class at any time, and to understand what constitutes good progress for the full range of children. Some children know when they are learning well, usually because it is self-evident, but others, most often the slower learners, but also many boys, need to have their progress made clear to them. The whole-class summary session at the end of the literacy hour was useful for this purpose, provided time was protected to use it well. It should be retained for phonics lessons.

■ **Children learn to spell the words they learn to read**: The more children understand from the outset that reading and writing is a two-way process, in which they use letters to compose words as well as to read them, the more chance they have of making accurate spelling a habit. The research from Clackmannanshire was particularly positive on the effects of phonics on spelling – 11-year-old girls and boys had a much greater advantage in spelling than in any other part of the research. Spelling is discussed in detail in Chapter 5, but some of the following short activities should be included in every phonics lesson:

- Making words from plastic letters, on desk tops or magnetic boards.

- Writing words on small whiteboards.

- Giving children a series of squares, into which they insert letters or groups of letters:

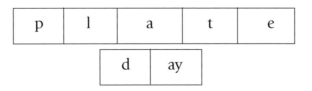

- Hangman (using words learned in the lesson).

- Finding other words with the same spelling pattern (using dictionary).

■ **There are good personal relationships, and a good pace of work**: Children need to know that you understand what they find easy and difficult, and that you are with them all the way in both areas. Praise is crucial, and needs to be used with precision so that it reinforces learning – it is essential not to patronise a struggling learner by praising things that are not quite right. In these cases, praise the effort and indicate clearly what needs to be worked on. A good pace of work is necessary for these children to see that they are making progress and understand what they do. Above all – and this is perhaps an unusual point to make in the context of relationships – you need yourself to know the ins and outs of spelling in enough detail to know where the difficulties are, which children are likely to run into them, and what will be the best way of presenting them to minimise stress. Your command of the subject either inspires confidence in children or saps it. The contribution of teaching assistants is crucial, and to do their work properly they also need to understand spelling patterns in the same detail as teachers.

■ **The lesson is well timed, and does not last too long**: A lesson is well timed if it maximises learning, and twenty minutes to half an hour is often plenty, particularly for younger children. A lesson format of introduction, explanation, practice and review is a good starting point, but should not be a straitjacket, and your judgement on timing is crucial. Sometimes an extra session of reinforcement with games is best timed just before the children go home, or just after lunch, or even at registration time. The important question is not what the teacher does in each session, or how long it lasts, but how well the children learn in it. The need for what has been called a 'discrete' – that is, separate – phonics lesson does not imply that phonic work needs to be taught in isolation, but simply that there needs to be a distinct and separate lesson for it each day. Short periods of reinforcement can be fitted into any lesson. An idea from Ruth Miskin is 'Fred Talk' (see box below).

Fred Talk

Fred is an imaginary character, who cannot speak in whole words, but has to break each word down into its constituent sounds. Fred talk is funny, and using it from time to time during the *d-ay h-e-l-p-s* children to hear the distinct sounds represented by letters in day-to-day speech. As in this example, of a single sound represented by a group of two or more letters, it is the sound that is pronounced and not the individual letters.

Resources are well chosen for their contribution to learning

Resources are important for what they do, rather than what they are. Sometimes the right resource is a blank playing card, or even a series of slips of paper that are written on to provide instant pin-point reinforcement or support. Sometimes an expensive resource, such as an interactive whiteboard, holds the interest of children whose attention might wander, and gives them a sense of involvement as they take their turn to make a correct selection and be praised in front of the class. The co-ordinator needs to know about all of the available resources in order to advise and support colleagues in their choice. This takes time, and involves attending educational exhibitions to see new resources, as well as reading or writing reviews in the educational press and teachers' television programmes. Resources are reviewed in Chapter 7, but each teacher should have access to the following resources.

Resources checklist

■ A good core scheme with a clear scheme of work.

■ Additional books, matched to the different reading levels in the class.

■ An interactive whiteboard, to engage pupils and encourage participation.

■ Informal resources, including blank cards, magnetic boards and letters.

■ Games to reinforce specific aspects of learning .

■ Small whiteboards for children to use, with markers and cleaning equipment.

■ Flipchart or whiteboard.

■ A Language Master machine, to feed back to children the sound of their own voice reading words, and to compare this with the teacher's.

All children have work they can understand and are fully involved

Infant teachers are skilled in managing class lessons to involve all children, for example, by using talk partners to discuss questions so that everyone answers a question, and by using small whiteboards for informal writing, so that the teacher can see at a glance everyone's attempt at a word or sentence. Good assessment will show which children are likely to find an idea difficult; they can be helped by working closely with teaching assistants to introduce the work in advance of the lesson rather than afterwards. This gives the child a head-start in making sense of the work, and avoids the error of putting in support after the child has failed. If children are still unable to learn effectively, it is much better for them to work individually or in groups with assistants who can put in all of the modification that they need rather than to sit in confusion and possibly misbehave.

What should teaching assistants do?

The main difference between the roles of the teacher and the teaching assistant is that the assistant tends to work with individual children and groups, and spends most of his or her time with children for whom learning is not straightforward. Other than this, teachers' and assistants' work is very similar.

Assistants' training needs are discussed in Chapter 8; for the moment, we will assume that, in relation to the children they work with, assistants:

- know and understand phonic patterns and major irregular features in English

- know the school's core scheme and resources in sufficient detail

- know and understand the learning difficulties they are working with

- understand and know how to use the school's agreed teaching methods

- know how these can be modified to meet individual learning needs

- know and understand record keeping and assessment systems

- have good personal relationships and can engage children in their work.

With these skills, the assistant can and should:

- discuss planning with the teacher, to see how far their children's needs can be met in the context of the normal lesson, and what modifications may be needed.

- anticipate snags, and plan in advance to counter them

- provide support, wherever possible, for potential difficulties before children meet them

- develop additional resources, games and explanations for difficult points

- set clear and realistic targets, and assess progress towards them

- keep informal records to pinpoint progress and the exact cause of problems.

Central to this approach is the idea that assessment will tell us which children are likely to have problems with new material, or need additional work on using their memories effectively. If we anticipate these difficulties, and set aside time for them on a systematic basis, we maximise children's chances of making sense of the work in the class lesson, and hence learning from it. In some schools, the system used in *Read, Write Inc.*, in which assistants regularly provide extra teaching to groups of children in the afternoon on the basis of work done in the morning, will be a good starting point, though in my experience preparing the children for work to come is at least as important as going over things again. Assessment should, however, also show which children are not making the progress they need to even after group help, and individual teaching can be added flexibly as need be. This is likely to be much more cost-effective than signing children up for expensive, long courses of individual teaching using a set formula.

How do we track progress?

Assessment needs to support teaching, and should be as compact as possible. The scheme of work and graded books provide a clear and simple basis for keeping track of the progress of most of the class. Normal professional judgement should be used, based on children's answers to questions and their ability to apply what they have learned to see whether a concept has been understood or whether it needs more work. There is no need to write all of this down. Individual reading records can be built into a home–school reading scheme as detailed below.

Home–school reading record

A small notebook accompanies each child's current book, which goes home each night in a stout bag with the school's logo. Teachers, assistants and parents or carers all use it, signing each entry. As the child reads, they make a note of any words that the child gets stuck on or hesitates over. If possible, they add some similar words – words with similar endings are often best – and provide help. Over time, the booklet generates a running record of points of difficulty, and provides a quick checklist that any adult can use to check if the child has learned the words or needs more help with them. Overall comments on the reading can be added, from either the adults or children. These booklets can become a most effective vehicle for dialogue and co-operation between the school, pupils, parents or carers.

Tracking fast progress

Extend the core scheme by building up a selection of key texts, possibly graded, that you and your colleagues know children will enjoy, and that develop particular skills. *The Lighthouse Keeper's Lunch* (Armitage and Armitage 1994) enjoyed by the Nabbotts Infant School children, for example, has demanding vocabulary, but short paragraphs. It is also well illustrated, so that it makes interesting reading for a mature 6- or 7-year-old. Extension materials should include non-fiction, simple biographies and short science texts, and children should be encouraged to use the junior and public libraries if the infant library is too simple for them. It is important to keep children's age and interests in mind, and not stretch them in too many directions at once. More demanding texts contain more complex phonic patterns, which can be taught as they arise. Able readers can often spot patterns in new words, and they should be encouraged to investigate them. A talking dictionary – the *Concise Oxford English Dictionary* is a very good one – allows them to enter words and hear them pronounced correctly.

Assessment for weaker readers and spellers

Assessing reading

Assessment needs to be made from direct observation. Photocopying (copyright permitting) a single page of a child's book and making notes on it is an economic way of recording reading. The text tells you what the child has read accurately, and a note of errors or words refused above the word or in the margin allows you to compare it with the original word. If the photocopy includes a picture, it may show the picture as the source of the error. There is no point, incidentally, in ticking every word the child gets right – this is recorded by the text itself, as no error is noted. Repeating the procedure at suitable intervals – from three months to a year, depending on the pupil and the nature of the difficulties – allows an informal record of progress that stands alongside the core record and any national tests or other assessments. This record is very useful for explaining a child's problem to parents, as it allows you to show exactly what is going wrong, and why. If it is not possible to photocopy the page, for copyright or other reasons, use the same procedure but make notes in a notebook. A clear reference to the original will enable you to put the notes and text together. You may wish to add a summary note.

Points to look for when assessing reading

■ What is the child getting right without hesitation?

■ What words does the child hesitate over, and can he or she work them out?

■ Does the child correct any of his or her own mistakes? (This is often the most positive sign of progress, as it shows growing control.)

■ What kinds of words are being misread? Are they mostly short, irregular words, or longer words, which may not be in the child's vocabulary, or a mixture? If a mixture, what words are in the mix?

■ Is the child reading accurately any words that have previously caused problems?

■ Is there any interference from shortcuts taken in everyday speech?

> ■ Does the child show signs of distress when reading? These can include reluctance to look at the page, avoidance strategies, including misbehaviour, complaints of headaches, furrowed brows, excessive blinking or screwing up eyes.

A short assessment such as this can honestly be presented to the child as an activity to tell us what we need to teach. Teaching techniques for the difficulties described above are included in Chapter 8. Two further tests, however, may be very useful in specific cases:

- **Intuitive Overlays Testing Pack**: available from the Institute of Optometry (www.ioo.org.uk at £50). A small but significant minority of children are held up in the early stages of learning to read by visual discomfort, which may be worse under fluorescent lighting. Some of these children will not have experienced any visual problems before they begin to read, as reading places new demands on the visual system – children have not only to focus closely, but need to move their eyes systematically to track the text. This screening kit allows you to see whether children who are experiencing discomfort might benefit from using a coloured overlay. It is simple to use, and supplies of overlays are available from the Institute of Optometry. If visual discomfort is the root cause of a reading problem, a great deal of trouble can be saved by this simple check.

- **British Picture Vocabulary Scale**: published by NFER-NELSON (www.nfer-nelson.co.uk at £135). Children are shown a series of sets of four pictures, while the teacher reads a word. They pick the picture that corresponds most closely to the word. A simple test, taking 5 to 8 minutes, this can give valuable information on children's understanding of words. It is particularly helpful for children who are not active speakers, or who have English as an additional language.

Assessing spelling

Spelling is easily tracked by keeping samples of children's work and noting, perhaps with a marker, words that are correctly spelled and the frequency and nature of errors. This is more effective than spelling tests, as these do not test spelling in the context of writing; when children write, they have to give much of their attention to their meaning, and the need to divide their attention makes spelling much more difficult when writing than it is when taking a spelling test. The points below should appear clearly from an analysis of a piece of writing, and can be used to help children develop individual strategies to avoid their own errors. This approach can be used equally with weak and very strong spellers.

Points to look for in assessing spelling

- What is the child getting right? Look for patterns in correct spelling as well as individual words.
- Is there any individual pattern to the spelling errors?
- How accurate is the child on vowels, both single and vowels that are written with a group of two or more letters? Which vowels or groups are causing problems?
- How accurate is the child on other combinations, such as *ck* at the end of words?
- Is there accurate use of more advanced combinations and groups, such as *ce, ci, cy, ge, gi, gy, tion*?
- Is the child inserting extra letters where they are not needed?
- Are there errors with double letters?
- (In discussion with the child) Is the child avoiding writing words he or she is not sure of spelling?
- Is spelling held up by weak handwriting?

FURTHER READING

Foundations of Literacy, Sue Palmer and Ros Bayley (2004) Stafford: Network Educational Press. A colourful and imaginative companion to early language development, with many practical suggestions.

Reading through Colour, Arnold Wilkins (2003) Chichester: Wiley. An authoritative survey of research into sensitivity to light in relation to reading and headaches.

HAPTER 3

Synthetic Phonics and Language Development

This chapter will:

- Describe and update Vygotsky's theory of language development
- Consider differences in early language experience
- Describe the influence of nursery rhymes on language
- Show how phonics help the transition between spoken language and literacy
- Discuss ways of tackling the shortcuts we take in everyday speech
- Consider how phonics help children begin modern languages

Vygotsky on early language development

The Russian psychologist L. S. Vygotsky died under Stalinist persecution in 1934, and his work was only published in the West some thirty years later. His two best-known works are *Thought and Language* (1986) and *Mind in Society* (1987).

The most important part of *Thought and Language* is the concept of 'inner speech'. Vygotsky began by investigating the ways in which children up to the age of around seven appeared to talk to themselves, a phenomenon that had been noticed by Piaget. Vygotsky found that the amount of this talk doubled when children had some kind of task to complete, and that what they said was related to the task – they were, in effect, talking themselves through it:

'Where's the pencil? I need a blue pencil. Never mind, I'll draw with the red one and wet it with water; it will become dark and look like blue.' (1986:16)

He concluded that the habit of talking to themselves did not simply wither on the vine as children grew older, but moved inwards, so that, most of the time, they talked things through inside their heads rather than out loud.

This pattern continued into adulthood, so that, in Vygotsky's analysis, language operates on three levels:

- inner speech, which only has to be clear to ourselves, and in which we take all manner of personal shortcuts

- speech, in which we communicate with others orally

- written speech, which operates through symbols.

For Vygotsky, inner speech and speech were examples of 'spontaneous concepts', developing naturally, while written speech was an 'artificial' or 'non-spontaneous' concept, that required communication through symbols, and had to be specifically taught in school. The development of 'written speech' followed a different pattern from speech itself; it was difficult in the initial stages, particularly writing, which children in his view could not easily see the point of, but led to the mastery of more complex structures and of what he called 'deliberate structure of the web of meaning'. Writing, said Vygotsky,

> requires deliberate analytical action on the part of the child. In speaking, he is hardly conscious of the sounds he pronounces, and quite unconscious of the mental operations he performs. In writing, he must take cognisance of the sound structure of each word, dissect it, and reproduce it in alphabetical symbols, which he must have studied and memorised before. In the same deliberate way, he must put written words together to form a sentence. (1986: 182)

The discovery of inner speech has stood the test of time, and is reflected in all of our experience. We have language in our minds whether we are speaking, listening, reading, writing or just sitting by ourselves. The flexibility of this inner speech allows us to organise our thoughts, and to edit them – none of us says everything we think. However, the language of inner speech is full of shortcuts, and has to be made progressively more elaborate as we communicate our meaning to others. Where we are in an intimate, family context, a high level of shared meaning means that much can be left unsaid – this can be an obstacle to education if parents go too far towards allowing children to communicate by means of gestures and sounds rather than making their meaning clear in words. In the courtroom or lecture hall, though, spoken language, can be just as formal and elaborated as written language, and is in some ways more demanding, as it takes place in 'real time'. On paper, we can make alterations if we find a better way of saying something, whereas a wrong word cannot always be taken back once it is spoken.

Vygotsky's theories: an update

Vygotsky's discovery of inner speech is one of the greatest linguistic achievements of the twentieth century. Nevertheless, modern investigations of the development of speech in family contexts, using technology that was not available to Vygotsky, have shown that his idea that speech is spontaneous, and writing artificial, is too simple. Speech is modelled and taught, either formally or informally, by parents, carers and other adults. Evidence of the importance of teaching speech comes both from common experience – how many children 'spontaneously' develop the practice of saying *please* and *thank you* – and from research, which shows great variations in the practices of different groups of parents, as well as a growing problem with interference to language development from exposure to media. No single research study covers all of the relevant issues, but the following are among the most important.

Barbara Tizard and Martin Hughes (1984) investigated the language used in the hour after lunch each day by two groups of fifteen mothers and their daughters. One group had left school without qualifications, while the other had husbands who held high-status jobs (apparently implying that these mothers had been successful in their own education). The researchers found important differences between the groups. The better-educated parents tended to require their children to make their meaning clear rather than to interpret what the child was trying to say, and took a positive attitude to questions, welcoming them and trying to answer them fully. The less educationally successful mothers

> ... seemed to place less stress on introducing their young daughters to a wide range of general knowledge and information and extending their vocabulary, and on giving them adequate answers whenever they asked questions. On the other hand, some seemed to place more stress on helping their daughters to acquire domestic and mothering skills. (1984: 159)

The authors interpreted these contrasts as 'differences in style', but this is a euphemism. Negative attitudes to questions in particular are likely to lead to fewer questions being asked, and hence to inhibit curiosity.

Betty Hart and Todd Risley (2003) considered the impact of different parental approaches in a study of forty-two families in the United States. They found that, by the age of three, children in professional families were hearing more language, and of greater variety, than those in families described as working class, and that there was a further gap between children in working class families and those whose parents were receiving welfare benefits. The number of words heard per hour was 616 for Welfare recipients' children, 1,251 for working-class children, and 2,153 for the children of professional families. The researchers found these figures reflected in the quality of the children's own language: 'When we listened to the children, we seemed to hear their parents speaking' (Ross et al. 2006: 44). The issue of encouragement was perhaps even more important. The children of Welfare recipients typically heard five instances of encouragement and eleven prohibitions or reprimands per hour. Those of the professional parents heard thirty-two encouragements and five negative comments. Extrapolated to the first four years of life, this amounts to 560,000 more positive than negative comments for the child of professional parents, and 125,000 more negative than positive comments for the child of parents receiving welfare.

The large-scale Bristol Child Development Study (Wells 1987) in the 1980s found that these differences were reflected in children's success and failure in school. The child who was most successful in school at eleven had had 5,000 recorded experiences of books, stories and nursery rhymes at home, while the child who was least successful had none at all. The late Dr Sally Ward (1994) found a further complication when working with the Manchester Central Health Care Trust in the early 1990s. Health visitors started reporting an unusu-ally high incidence of young children who did not respond either to sounds they heard or to the human voice. Might they be deaf? A study of 1,000 chil-dren aged nine months to one year showed that they were not, but were so heavily exposed to media of various types that their normal communicative instincts had become impaired. Dr Ward developed a system of early interven-tion to help parents to deal with the problem, which involved an average of four individual visits from a speech therapist. This produced very substantial improvements, which were still apparent in 3-year-old children, and initial investigations also suggest that the benefits have been carried on into school.

Dr Ward identified the use of television and videos as babysitters, even among better-off parents who employ nannies, as a major problem, and it is easy to see why. Individual conversation with a baby or young child is a two-way process, in which the adult naturally adopts his or her words and tone of voice to the indi-vidual needs and response of the infant. The very pace of this language may well be crucial. Videos and taped music proceed at one speed, and take no notice of whether the audience is smiling or crying. Peter Hobson (2002), a professor of developmental psychopathology at Harvard, suggests that early communication takes the form of a triangle, with parent and child at two of the corners, observing and discussing the world. The intrusion of media breaks this pattern, isolating the child and pouring language into him or her without any expectation of response. Sue Palmer, in *Toxic Childhood* (2006), provides evidence from Germany and Japan that indicates that the phenomenon of media interfering with early language development is not confined to English-speaking countries. Nevertheless, with the pattern of long hours of work and concentrated social problems in some areas, the problems caused by over-exposure to media are particularly serious in British schools. Additional activities for children whose early language development causes concern are given in Chapter 2.

CASE STUDY

Speech deprivation in a South London nursery

The nursery was attached to a primary school in an outer suburb, and served a large area of public housing. Almost no parents had experience of higher education; there were high levels of unemployment and some drug-taking. Staff observed that most children joined the nursery at three or four with very little understanding of the use of language for communication, and used very few words. Much of the nursery's work therefore focused on creating contexts in which children would begin to experience meaningful communication. They would be taken to visit various members of staff, including the school secretary, and would learn to greet them politely and use words rather than gestures to express themselves. The structures of the nursery were based on involving the children in the use of language, whatever they chose to do, and on creating contexts in which they would feel comfortable in responding through words. As the conditions that had led to the problem remained in place throughout the children's school career, lessons in the main school continued to be adapted to building language, with carefully designed materials that asked questions and rewarded thoughtful response. This led to very good teaching and consistently effective learning. Even so, the school's test results at seven and eleven remained well below national average levels.

Using nursery rhymes, with actions

Any story or nursery rhyme involves a length and complexity of language that is much greater than children meet or use if language is confined to managing everyday situations and communicating needs and wants. At the beginning, children often speak in single words or clusters of two or three phrases, whereas most nursery rhymes have strings of twenty to forty words, and a dynamic, grammatical structure that takes a child out of its immediate context and involves a kind of mental dialogue.

Consider the range of verb forms and tenses, for example, in *Oranges and Lemons*, or even:

Three blind mice,
Three blind mice,
See how they run,
See how they run.
They ran right over the farmer's wife.
She cut off their tails with a carving knife.
Did you ever see such a thing in your life
As three blind mice?

Adding actions gives children a physical involvement in the work, and may help those who are most reluctant to speak. Tommy, whom we met in Chapter 1, would join in with actions to *Arabella Miller* with great energy as well as shouting out the words. It may have been the security of the structure and rhythm that helped overcome his inhibitions.

Phonics and the transition to literacy

Dame Marie Clay refines Vygotsky's idea of literacy as a non-spontaneous concept in her description of becoming literate as 'the construction of inner control' (Clay 1991). Phonics plays a key part in this process by making the representation of the sounds of words explicit, so that it can be controlled and applied deliberately to the task of reading and constructing words. The blending and word-building features of synthetic phonics are crucial to developing this control, as simply noting features, as in the analytic phonics approach, does not enable the children to apply what they have learned.

Once children have read or spelled a word using this approach, they then consolidate it by practice. Seen in this way, Frank Smith's famous comment, 'We learn to read by reading' (1994: 169) has a grain of truth. Each succeeding time children meet a word they have worked out, they do not have to construct it from scratch, but retrieve the information from the letters with increasing ease. With time, the process becomes, to the naked eye, so fast that it appears automatic. As we recognise more and more words, we are able to pay more attention to the meaning of what we read. Professor Katharine Perera's doctoral research (1989) found that children only began to group words into phrases in their reading after they were reading accurately at a rate of sixty to seventy words per minute. It is simply not possible to sound words out at a rate of one or more a second, but it is possible to retrieve them at that rate, using what the letters tell us and the information stored in our memory.

Words that children are able to read without consciously working them out are often referred to as 'sight vocabulary'. However, this reflects earlier limitations in the equipment used to monitor the way the eyes work as we read, and not what is actually happening. Scanning equipment that records the activity of each eye separately shows much finer focusing and tracking than has been detected by earlier technology, and indicates that the reader is paying attention not only to each word and each letter, but also to the details that distinguish one letter from another. This intense visual activity does not happen by chance, and indicates that retrieving information from print involves processes of visual and intellectual discrimination that were hidden from the theorists who reasoned that we read so quickly that we could not possibly be paying this level of attention to detail. The speed of the process, and its intricacy, can be seen in the examples of long words that are distinguished only by their final letters. To read and pronounce accurately *photograph, photographic, photography, photographer*, we need to use our eyes, our knowledge of the root word, and our understanding of variations in pronunciation. The presence or absence of one or two letters, which are phonically regular, makes all the difference.

CASE STUDY

Language into phonics – Mapledene Early Years Centre, Hackney

Most children at Mapledene are aged two to four, and many speak a language other than English at home. Janet Taylor, head of the centre, and teacher Kirsteon Harron have built up a programme of continuous development of their awareness of language that leads naturally into phonics. They begin with awareness of pattern in sound, using and repeating sounds, stories, rhythms, patterns and music, and emphasising the sounds in children's names to involve them. As children begin to predict text in stories, such as *Mr Magnolia* (Blake 1999) or *We're Going on a Bear Hunt* (Rosen and Oxenbury 2003), the rhyme and rhythm in the prediction helps them recognise phonic patterns. Once children hear the rhythm and melody of words, they are encouraged to pick out words with initial sounds, playing 'I-spy' with teachers and parents.

With children between the ages of two-and-a-half to three-and-a-half, teachers gradually take a more structured approach, deliberately incorporating specific sounds into lessons. By the time they are four, when learning activities across the centre become more focused, children learn to break words down and build them up throughout the day. Words are chosen from whatever else is going on – the heart pumping blood around the body will lead to short, lively activities acting out the pumping. At the same time, focusing attention on shapes helps children understand the shapes in letters.

Using Montessori principles, Kirsteon begins with two letters whose shapes are very different, both visually and in the sound they represent. One is normally the first letter of their name. Children trace these letters using the first two fingers of their dominant hand. Adults then increase each child's knowledge of the significance of these letters in the environment, using sand trays, chalks and other systems. Once these are secure, Kirsteon extends the range of letters, ensuring that there is a personal interest or connection with each new letter – for example, a child interested in dinosaurs would learn the initial *d*, and, later the *s*. Letters would be picked out from other dinosaurs names or from other interests – *B* for *Barbie*, for example.

Once children have awareness of most of the alphabet, attention focuses on the initial sounds of words. Kirsteon has a box of items including a cat, mat, bus, sun, and children are encouraged to pick out the intial letters and then other sounds. A

▶

popular game is the phonic crocodile — each wrong guess takes the children one step closer to an imaginary pond, in which lurks a crocodile. Kirsteon also has the children chalk circles and shapes on the floor. She calls out letters, sounds or names — children need both, but it is a matter of judgement as to when and how these are introduced — and the children jump into the shapes. After children are confident with initial sounds, the focus moves to final, and then middle sounds in words.

Children then have simple books that Kirsteon has made herself. The first have pictures, for example, of balls bouncing, with the letter *b* printed on the page. Children colour the picture and talk about the letter with an adult. Their progress is recorded using a simple triangle system — one stroke when the letter is introduced, a second when they recognise it with support, and the third when they pick it out confidently. Kirsteon presents up to three letters at a time, depending on the child's understanding. The second books introduce middle and final sounds using three-letter words and pictures. Adults take care to pronounce all parts of each word clearly, and particularly to enunciate the final letter, especially if it is one that is likely to be dropped, such as *cat*. Kisteon considers this crucial to children with special educational needs and to those with English as an additional language — if they don't hear a letter, they will not know they need to write it. The third book moves on to words with more than three letters, combinations such *sh*, *ch*, *ck*, and simple sentences.

Once children know some high-frequency words at sight, they are encouraged to combine them to make simple phrases and sentences. Where letters don't behave as expected, Kirsteon warns the children to watch out, or they will trick them. Tricky letters include the final *e* in cake, and the *ph* in elephant. Kirsteon makes a game out of the idea of tricky letters. At each stage Kirsteon ensures that children fully understand what they are working on before introducing new material.

Neighbouring schools say that children arrive with a high level of understanding of sounds and letters, and that gifted and talented children make outstanding progress. The centre responds flexibly to this — one child was able to tackle a Year 2 national test paper before starting school, and passing this information to the school allowed her to be placed on the gifted and talented register from the reception class.

Phonics and everyday speech

In Vygotsky's model, inner speech is full of shortcuts and infinitely flexible. As soon as we speak, we have to make our meaning clear to at least one other person. We still take shortcuts, depending on how well we know whoever we are speaking to, how much verbal and non-verbal feedback we receive, and how much they will do to interpret what we say as we mean to say it, rather than require us to make our meaning explicit. The concept of a shortcut is valuable to the literacy teacher as it is socially neutral. Members of all social classes take shortcuts when they speak, and, while some take more than others, the basic facts of saving time and communicating effectively are common to all. The most frequent shortcut taken by all English speakers is the indistinct pronunciation of some voice sounds, so that the final a sound we hear in the English pronunciation of, say, *animal* or *capital*, is much less distinct than in their original French, in which the second a is pronounced as distinctly as the first. This shortcut is so universal that we have to use more than phonic information to ensure that we learn it effectively. The issue is discussed in Chapter 5.

Shortcuts may take place at the word and sentence level. At the sentence level, they involve grammatical shortcuts, often taken in non-Standard English. For example, a speaker of Black London English once said to me, referring to a local health centre, 'It all right. Me go there yesterday.' There is no mistaking the sense, and the shortcuts are grammatical. The first sentence omits the verb *to be*, the second uses *me* rather than *I*, and *yesterday* is the only marker for the past tense. Learning to take shortcuts such as these in childhood makes the route to formal written English a longer and more difficult one, but the concept of a shortcut enables it to be undertaken without underestimating the speaker's abilities or causing offence.

Shortcuts at the sentence level can also affect reading. Most of us speak in sentences that are shorter than those we would write, and most children certainly do. This can lead to them phrasing their reading in a way that stops at a word they might naturally stop at when speaking, even if this involves an error, when the writer has in fact continued to write something slightly more elaborate. For example, a 10-year-old I worked with recently misread:

in our bodies are thousands of chemicals …

for:

in our bodies are thousands of chemical reactions, that are crucial to life.

He came to a stop when he reached *reactions*, and could not make sense of it because of the train of meaning he had imposed on the previous word, simply by reading it as plural rather than singular. This type of error, which essentially foreshortens the sentence, becomes increasingly important as children move towards secondary school and is an important reason for teaching them to use all of the information provided by letters.

Shortcuts from everyday speech are a particular problem in spelling. If we can't hear a sound, or are not aware of hearing it, we have to reconstruct the word before we can spell it, and this is difficult. Most spelling errors involve leaving letters out rather than putting letters in, particularly in words such as *probably* which is easily misspelled as *probly*, *different* as *difrent*. Strategies for dealing with such shortcuts are considered in Chapter 5.

Pause for reflection ...

I often ask children if, when they need to write a word they're not sure of spelling, they choose another word instead. Most do, and some university students have said that they will even rewrite a sentence to avoid using a word they're not sure of spelling. The only conclusion from this is that weak spelling limits many people's capacity to express themselves in writing — instead of writing what they want to write, they write what they can spell.

The first step to take to investigate this question is to ask the children or students you teach if they avoid using words they're not sure of spelling, and to base your strategy on their answers, and on the evidence of their work. If you find children are doing this, you need to find a way of helping them to take the risk.

Possible strategies include having them write what they know of a word, with a line underneath it to draw it to your attention for explanation, and giving positive rewards for adventurous and interesting vocabulary — Training materials from the National Literacy Strategy called them *premier league* words — whether or not the word is correctly spelled. You can then use Slimmed Down Spelling to explain the features of the words, and encourage the children to find some more that are like them.

FURTHER READING

Thought and Language, L. S. Vygotsky (1986) Boston: MIT. Chapter 6. Vygotsky's insights into language development and the transition to literacy are still of great value, and his original version is essential reading.

Mind in Society, L. S. Vygotsky (1987) Cambridge, MA: Harvard University Press. Vygotsky's second collection published in English has been influential on the social context of literacy; it should not be read in isolation from *Thought and Language*.

On Common Ground, Jill Pirrie (1994) Godalming: WWF. Jill Pirrie's approach to teaching poetry, which she also used in teaching non-fiction writing, illustrates the new dimension literacy brings to language development through having children reflect on and develop their initial thoughts. The focus on what is important, and why, is essential.

CHAPTER 4

How Do We Explain and Tackle Irregularity?

This chapter will:

■ Describe the effects of irregularity, and of shortcuts taken in everyday speech

■ Consider the French connection in more detail

■ Introduce the concept of fuzzy logic as a description of English spelling.

■ Describe the most important irregular patterns

■ Introduce teaching techniques that enable children to deal with irregularity

Effects of irregularity

Irregularity makes learning to read and spell more difficult in English than in very regular languages. But how much more difficult? And how does the problem show itself at different stages of learning to read, and for different groups of children and adults? In order to explain irregularity, and to teach children how to tackle it, we need to understand it and its effects in some detail.

Irregularity causes particular problems for children in the earliest stages of reading, when they have very limited knowledge of the alphabetic system and no store of words in their memory that they can read without working them out from scratch. Rose (2006: 18) says that, as English is not fully regular, many children are unlikely to pick out phonic patterns for themselves. This point can be extended to say that as phonics do not always work, children also have to be taught how to read words when phonics do not apply.

Professor Steven Pinker (1999) notes in his work on irregular verbs that they tend to be words of very high frequency, and he suggests that they are therefore learned by heart rather than by applying rules. This point appears to extend beyond verbs. We have only to look at the high proportion of the most common English words that are irregular to see that frequency can be an asset – words that are used very frequently come up a lot, so that children get a lot of practice with them. Learning by heart, though, is not a straightforward option. Children with reading difficulties almost always have weaknesses in the way they use their memories. If they are to learn effectively, memory work needs to be carefully structured, with difficulties anticipated and clear patterns reinforced. Chapter 8 includes a practical approach to memory work.

As children make progress, the balance of what they do and do not understand changes. They learn to adjust their thinking to use simple groups of letters, such as *th*, *sh* and *ch*, and to accommodate words in which letters give them different information in different contexts – *i* in *fish* and *file*, for example. Almost all learn to recognise at least some of the least regular words through sheer repetition, though this can't be taken for granted. The most successful children see for themselves similarities both in regular words and in irregular words, such as *some* and *come*. The more clearly children see, understand and practise the regular patterns in the language, the more oddities stick out, and able readers often pick up and apply patterns in them for themselves. More complex regular patterns, such as the softening effect of *e*, *i* and *y* on *c* and *g*, also require an adjustment in children's thinking, but this extends their repertoire of patterns and is different in nature from, for example, learning how to use the particularly irregular group *ough*, which can give several different sounds. As children move towards secondary school, they meet an increasing number of words derived from Latin and Greek. These words have a high degree of regularity, so that the proportion of irregular words they meet is probably lower than that encountered by beginning readers, and certainly no higher.

Pause for reflection ...

- How well do the children you teach deal with irregularity?
- Are there any groups of children who tackle it particularly well or badly?
- What are the main strengths and weaknesses of these groups?
- What techniques and strategies do you use to help your pupils?
- How effective are they, and for which groups of children?
- If they are not fully effective, what might be done to improve them?

Irregularity and everyday speech

We have seen in Chapter 1 that the main causes of irregularity in English are the Norman conquest of 1066 and the major shifts in pronunciation, particularly of voice sounds, in the Middle Ages. In practical terms, we also need to consider the growing mismatch between spelling and everyday speech. This takes two main forms: omitting sounds, usually *t,* at the ends of words, and blurring pronunciation, both of vowels and consonants. A secondary home economics teacher in Essex once asked me to teach her class *stool,* with which her room was equipped. Half the class wrote it as *stall,* and it was clear from discussion with the students that they did not make any distinction between the two words in speech. A frequent shortcut with consonants is to pronounce *th* as *f* – this is long established in London dialect, and not due to Estuary English. *Th* takes more work to pronounce, as the tongue has to be placed between the teeth and withdrawn, while *f* requires just a touch of the lips. Shortcuts such as these save time, but blur in speech a distinction that children later have to observe in writing, so that children who take such shortcuts have to work harder to spell accurately.

Dr Johnson and the printers

Dr Johnson is often blamed for the irregularity of English spelling, but printers had already introduced and made permanent some of the most awkward spelling groups before he wrote his *Dictionary* (1755). These include the notorious *ough,* which represents several different sounds: *thought, through, enough, although, thorough, plough, cough.* The following two errors, from Dr Johnson and the printer William Caxton, show how oddities have come to establish themselves in English spelling:

- ■ Dr Johnson: The verb *to ache* was originally written *ake,* like *make.* Dr Johnson thought it must have a connection with Greek, and so used *ch.* He was wrong. The *Oxford English Dictionary* says he was 'ignorant of the history of the word'. Ignorance has not prevented his word from becoming the correct spelling.

■ Caxton: Early spellings of *ghost* had no *h*. Caxton put one in, possibly taking it from the Flemish *gheest*. The *h* has no function, but the error is still accepted as the correct spelling.

These irregularities only affect a small part of a small number of words – apart from the *ch* and extra *h*, *ghost* and *ache* are regular. Unfortunately, no one has the authority to correct the errors, and so we are stuck with them.

Try this: teaching *ough*

ough is the most irregular pattern in English. However, the group *ough* makes a good pivot for teaching, as most of the words using it can be formed by remembering the group and adding letters. I sometimes ask a class to write *ough* several times down the middle of a page, and then add letters to make the words. The group can be chanted to the rhythm of a train, gradually speeding up. Words with a similar sound can then be grouped:

ought	thorough	plough
bought		bough
borough		Slough
thought		
fought		
brought	rough	though
(*optional*)	tough	dough
sought	enough	although
wrought		
		trough
		cough

The only word with no companion is *through*, which can be learned visually or by little phrases:

No through road.

I'm through with this.

He went straight through a red light.

In time, the group *ough* becomes as clearly established in the children's minds as a single letter. Using games and quizzes along the way makes the process enjoyable. The best starting point for this group is usually when a child needs or tries to use one of the words in writing. You can then teach other words with the same pattern as ▶

---

that one. This is likely to be at some point from Year 3 onwards, though some children may be curious about these words at a younger age. As the pattern is so irregular, it is a good idea to revisit it from time to time, extending the range of words for the higher-attaining children.

More on the French connection

The French connection operates in many different words and letter patterns. Roughly 30 per cent of the most common words are of French origin – a search of the *Oxford English Dictionary* produces 37,534.

The French connection: two examples

■ **Table:** The reason we spell table with the *l* before the *e* is rarely explained. Say *table* in French, and you can hear that *l* sounds clearly before *e*.

■ **Manger:** Most of us still know this word from the Christmas carol, though weak readers often misread it as *manager*. The French word for *to eat* is *manger* and animals eat from a manger. The connection is clear.

Understanding the French connection is an important part of children's mental map of English. Most of the Latinate vocabulary that children need in secondary school came through French. Moreover, the words can easily be turned back into French by changing the pronunciation, a huge boost to learning French. The following unit (also on the accompanying CD) can be used at any stage in the junior school, and should be reinforced over a term or so. The French connection is, though, much less frequent in the early stages of reading – of the DfES list for 7-year-olds, only *people* (from *peuple*) is obviously French.

How much irregularity is there?

Estimates of the regularity of the language vary from 50 to 85 per cent, depending on how it is calculated – it is impossible to be precise, as there is so much variation in the language different people use. For the child beginning reading, there is an additional complication from regular spelling that does not follow the most frequent pattern of letter–sound correspondence, and from shortcuts in spoken language. An early example is the two-letter combination (digraph) *th* in *the*. We can prepare children for these problems by explaining that letters do not always work on their own, but sometimes as a team, and that we sometimes have to think differently when we read and write from the way we think when we speak. All of us take shortcuts sometimes, but reading, and especially writing, have to be spelled out. If children are not alerted to their own shortcuts at an early stage, and in this socially neutral way, the issue is much harder to deal with later.

Irregular words in early reading

We define a word as irregular when it does not follow the most frequently occurring correspondence between its letters and sounds; the most frequent 100 words in English contain thirty-eight irregular words:

all, are, be, because, by, call, come, could, do, go, have, he, I, into, little, live, me, my, old, once, one, other, put, saw, said, she, so, some, their, there, they, to, today, two, was, were, what, you.

A further twenty-two words use combinations of letters – mostly vowel letters – that go beyond the straightforward pattern of a single sound for each letter:

about, away, back, came, down, here, like, look, made, make, new, now, our, out, see, take, the, that, this, three, time, with.

The DfES's list of forty-five high-frequency words for the reception year has fourteen irregular words, and there are forty-five in its list of 158 high-frequency words for Year 2.

Teaching the French connection

This unit aims to teach children the most common connections between French and English spelling, and how they came about. It can be taught in literacy lessons, in combination with the National Curriculum history on invaders and settlers. The unit also prepares children for studying French, by introducing the idea of changing pronunciation to read words that the languages have in common.

Starter: Write *table* on your whiteboards. Show me. Who has spelled it *table*? That's the correct spelling. Now, why do we spell it that way and not with the *e* before the *l*? (It is most unlikely that anyone will know the answer to this.) Now I'm going to say the word in French (pronounce it tab-*le*, with short *a*, emphasising, before *e*.) Can you hear that the *l* comes before the *e*? (Repeat until they all hear and understand.)

So, we have an English word with a spelling based on the way it sounds in French. Once we have the idea, we can make more words:

cable
stable
fable
able
noble

and some longer words:

capable
probable
possible
constable

(you might note that the vowel sound stays short in the longer words).

How did this happen? (See if any children have ideas, perhaps from their history lessons.) The answer is that in 1066, England was invaded by William the Conqueror, a very cruel man, who took over the whole country and gave it to his followers and soldiers. He could fairly be described as a bully. William and his people spoke French, and they were the bosses. Over the next 150 years, English became flooded with French words, and we still have a lot of them today – over 30,000, according to the *Oxford English Dictionary*.

Here are some more:

Manger (Write this on the board, and ask children to read it. You may need to clear up confusion with *manager*, as *manger* is not in most children's vocabulary. Explain that animals eat from it – I sometimes start to sing 'Away in a Manger' and stop to let them fill in the word, if they are likely to know it. I usually explain that, in the Bible story, they used a manger because they did not have a cot.) Once the children can read the word correctly in English, introduce the French word *manger*, to eat. Explain the link, and the way in which the meaning and pronunciation have altered.

Now look at these words:

danger
stranger
ranger
arrange
strange.

Now give the children this list of words, compiled by Canadian scholar Henri Seguin.

-age: bandage, image, page, message, usage, voltage, passage
-ance: chance, balance, finance, alliance, tolerance, ambulance
-ence: confidence, evidence, intelligence, providence, licence
-tion: nation, action, attention, administration, station

-al:	animal, normal, signal, cardinal, final, original, national
-ial:	racial, social, special, commercial, colonial, initial
-et:	alphabet, buffet, budget, cricket, ticket, violet, secret
-ect:	intellect, direct, correct, aspect, respect, suspect
-in:	Latin, cousin, assassin, bulletin, florin, mandarin
-ain:	gain, grain, refrain, train, quatrain, certain, vain
-ent:	accent, recent, innocent, precedent, incident, president
-ant:	vacant, elegant, elephant, extravagant, descendant
-ive:	offensive, initiative, tentative, co-operative, intensive
-ine:	discipline, machine, morphine, Vaseline, routine, sardine
-ible:	possible, compatible, sensible, invisible, terrible.

Explain that French and English words often have the same spelling and meaning, even though they are pronounced differently. Read the list through, or have the children do so, then have the children practise reading them in groups, with help from the assistant if needed. If possible, read the words in French (or have a French speaking colleague or parent volunteer do so) and explain any differences in meaning. Most of the time, the meaning is identical, but not always. The French don't use *station* for a railway station – their word *gare*, and our nearest equivalent is *garage* – we park cars, they park trains! Using words they already know in English will therefore often help them in learning French, provided they understand that the approach, like almost everything else in language, does not work all the time.

Optional extension: If children take to this very easily, you might explain how some of the changes took place in English and French.

Estrange was a word in both languages. The French dropped the *s*, as they had stopped pronouncing it, giving the modern French word *étrange*. We dropped the *e* to make *strange*, though we kept it for the now little used word *estrange*, meaning to lose touch. Similarly, we now have stranger, and the French word with the same meaning is *étranger*.

Serveral French and English words have moved in the same way – *étable* to *stable*, *établissement* to *establishment*.

The examples show how language users adapt the language to suit their own purposes.

Pause for reflection ...

■ Look at each of the thirty-eight irregular words listed on page 51. What adjust-
  ments or interpretation are needed to read each of them?

■ What patterns can you see in the irregular words? Can you think of other common
  words that share these patterns?

■ Which of these words do you find your children struggle with most? How do you
  help them, and what works best?

English spelling and fuzzy logic

Fuzzy logic is a branch of mathematical set theory, in which an item does not have
to contain all of the characteristics of a set in order to belong to it. Frank Smith
said that if English were phonically based, computers would be able to read text,
'to the great advantage of the blind' (1978: 51). Well, they can, and they use fuzzy
logic to do it. Essentially, the computer can construct words on the basis of imper-
fect, but consistent, information, and all of us have learned to do this too.

Sets may be based on spelling – *would, could, should* – or on word families, in
which emphasis or the pronunciation of a vowel may change without losing
membership of the group – *can, can't*. A similar path is taken in the contraction
of *shall not* to *shan't*. In all of these cases, we have to read the words on the basis
of what we know that the letters are telling us in these situations. Once we have
one word right, we may well be able to make analogies with others. Fuzzy logic
can be presented to children as a tool to help them to read and spell, provided
we do this in terms they can understand. Once they have grasped the mix of
logic and oddity in one word, others can be added to help them to learn by
analogy and to build up their mental map of the language.

Try this: irregular words

Before you use a new book with a class, pick out irregular words and teach them in
advance. As you read the book, draw attention to these words, and make games with
them from time to time.

This approach gives the children a clear run at a point of difficulty, rather than leaving them to work it out at the same time as they are giving their attention to the text
and its meaning.

Explaining spelling in terms of human nature

The quirks of English spelling make learning to read a personal matter – each of us has to make sense of the way spelling works, accommodating the oddities with the regularities. The goal of teaching is to make this easier, and to chart a course that enables the individual children we work with to tackle the problems with as much enjoyment and as little stress as possible.

From an early age, we have to adapt to other people's moods and behaviour, and this provides a useful way of introducing irregular features to children. Are they good all of the time or most of the time? Is mummy (or their teacher!) in a good mood all of the time or most of the time? Once they understand the idea that principles, including phonic principles, work most of the time, children and adult learners appreciate the help they give, and make allowances when they don't help as much as they would like. Such is life.

FURTHER READING

Alpha to Omega, Bevé Hornsby (1972) London: Heinemann. was the first book to analyse regular and irregular features in English spelling in detail. Its word lists are comprehensive and a most useful point of reference, particularly for more complex patterns. The book does not, however, explain how words have come to be irregular. Teachers interested in this should consult the *Oxford English Dictionary*, which is now available free, on line, via most public library tickets.

CHAPTER 5

Phonics and English Spelling

This chapter will:

- Review the phonic basis of the spelling system, including foreign elements and complications
- Outline the research in practical evidence that synthetic phonics is the basis of learning to spell
- Show how Slimmed Down Spelling enables children to use regular and irregular patterns in spelling
- Describe the main irregular patterns in English
- Introduce some key resources for teaching spelling

Synthetic phonics as the basis of spelling in English

As we write, we compose words with letters that correspond to the sounds we would make if we were saying the words aloud. The left-to-right movement when we write matches the order in which we pronounce the sounds, and we do not insert letters out of order. The basis of spelling is, therefore, phonic. We are representing sounds by letters, and we use synthetic phonics to compose the word. The visual system helps us to check whether a word looks right, and helps us to retain a mental picture of the word as we write it. The action of writing the words creates additional traces in the memory. Both of these, however, can only come into play after we have put the sounds together to make the word.

As we spell, however, we have to deal with the following snags:

- A significant number of words are based on foreign sound systems, particularly French.

- Pronunciation has changed over time, without any corresponding modification to the spelling system.

- We have different ways of representing the same and similar sounds.

- The shortcuts we take in everyday speech can make it difficult to hear the sounds in words clearly.

As teachers, we have to deal with the spelling we have and not the one we might like. The French have twice reformed their spelling to bring it closer to pronunciation, but they have an Academy with authority to do this, and no single country, let alone institution, now has such authority in English. To teach children to use the spelling we have, we need to enable them to use regular patterns, and to assimilate complex and irregular elements into this basic structure. They can only do this if they have a clear understanding of the basic features. If nothing is clear, we are in a state of confusion that inhibits every other aspect of writing and frequently causes distress. Weak spelling saps confidence, limits children 's power of expression, and is a major cause of disaffection and examination failure in secondary schools. Marking schemes for examinations that exclude spelling tackle the symptoms of the problem, and ignore both its causes and its broader psychological effects – if someone, child or adult, knows that everything they write is likely to be wrong, they will often be reluctant to write at all.

Try this: word avoidance

Ask a Year 6 class if they ever avoid using a word because they're not sure of its spelling. Then ask if they do this often, sometimes or rarely. Note the replies carefully, and see if there is any correspondence between how often children do this, and how well they spell. Analysing a sample of the writing of, say, two weak, average and strong spellers will then provide an indication of how effective your teaching of spelling is in the longer term. Use the results to identify which areas of spelling need more reinforcement through teaching.

Synthetic phonics and learning to spell

Dr Lynette Bradley's research (see, for example, Bradley and Bryant 1983) into children's awareness of patterns in sound showed that young children were often able to spell short words by combining letters before they could read them. This pattern of learning is also clear in Glenda Bissex's study *Gnys at Wrk* (1980). Despite the errors in this title, which will be discussed below, it is clearly an attempt to put down letters that represent what the child can hear, and two-thirds of it – all of the consonants and one vowel – are right. The research evidence from the Clackmannanshire study (Johnston and Watson 2005) is also particularly strong – specific teaching of using phonics for spelling led to an immediate and substantial gain in spelling skill that was sustained when children were seven, and was still present for both boys and girls – but particularly for boys – at eleven.

Rose (2006), however, emphasises that practical experience in schools is as important as research evidence. Both his team's visits to schools, and Ruth Miskin's (see www. readwriteinc.com) success in teaching spelling, both in her own inner-London school, and in other schools that have adopted her method, reflect increasing professional confidence in phonics as a basis for spelling. Once again, there is no contrary evidence of effective spelling teaching by other means.

Slimmed Down Spelling

The challenge for teachers is to enable children to deal with all aspects of spelling, and to do so in the context of writing, when they have to give most of their attention to what they want to say as well as taking care over punctuation and handwriting. To do this, the presentation of spelling needs to be simple, clear and accurate. It cannot present 'rules ' that are made unreliable by exceptions. Rules need to be reliable – it is a rule, for example, that we proceed from left to right in normal script and do not put letters out of order. It is not a rule that we use *i* before *e* except after *c* – there are too many exceptions in common words – *their, eight, height, weigh*. If we complicate the rule by relating it to different sounds, it presents children with too much to hold in their head at once. It is also important that we, as teachers, should not contradict ourselves by saying something we later change. Children trust us, and need to believe all we say, not just the last thing we have said.

I have developed Slimmed Down Spelling (see Bald 2001) in the course of over thirty years' experience of teaching people to spell, reviewing research for the *Times Educational Supplement* and *Education Guardian*, and training teachers. Many of the people I had worked with had suffered great anguish because of their spelling difficulties, which had placed an outright block on their achieving their potential at school and at work. I have always believed in high standards, but the extent to which a spelling difficulty can blight an intelligent person's life was and is unacceptable, and Jamie Oliver in particular has helped many people by smashing this barrier.

The problem seemed to start with weaknesses in the guidance and rules these learners had been given. Some, such as changing *y* to *i* before a plural – *sky*, *skies* – had hidden complications. This one did not work when there was a vowel before *y*, as in *day*, *days*, *key*, *keys*, and led to errors such as *skys* or *daies*. Others, like the *i before e* mentioned above, had simply too many exceptions. So, I tried to look at the question from the point of view of the writer who is not sure about his spelling and has to decide whether or not to include any letter. It seemed that the first thing we needed was a clear picture of the word in our mind, taking care to avoid the shortcuts that arise from everyday speech, as in the examples *probly* and *difrnt* in Chapter 3. Next, letters sometimes worked in groups, as in *ough*, *tion*, and it had been very helpful in teaching reading to focus on these groups and help children to use them to work out words. Some words had an extra letter. Often there was a reason for it. Bevé Hornsby's (1999) idea of a 'wall' to keep two vowels apart or to prevent *e* from softening *g*, as in *plague*, was very useful, but sometimes there was no basis in logic for the extra letter, as in *climb* and *thumb*. But there was usually only one extra letter in a word, even in a word as difficult as *chaos*, and if it could be isolated, then grouped with other words with the same extra letter, then the brain cells could form their own chunk and deal with these words.

The final piece in the jigsaw involved a return to shortcuts. It takes less effort to produce an indistinct vowel sound than to articulate it clearly, and it is human nature to economise on effort. Listen to modern, colloquial German and you will hear a softer, more flowing mode of speech than the harshness of the public speeches in the 1930s, resulting from less emphasis on articulation and more on getting meaning across easily. From the writer's point of view, this type of shortcut, in which the final *a* in a word such as *practical* is pronounced more as *e*, if it is pronounced at all, constitutes a distinct pattern that needs to be learned, as it cannot be deduced from the sound of a word in normal speech, even when it is carefully pronounced. The only compensation is that the problem only concerns one letter, and usually in the same position in a word, so that if we can spell *practical,* we can use the same learning for *central, optical, tropical* and so on. But we have to take care to use the pattern only when we've learned we need it. A pompous academic once felt the need to remind me that she was a princip*al* rather than a princip*le* lecturer.

Slimmed Down Spelling has helped many of my students to gain the confidence they need to express themselves in writing, and is simple enough for people to hold in their minds while their focus is on the meaning of what they write. It has the following key characteristics:

- It is simple, and easy for children to understand after a little practice.

- It is phonically based.

- It deals with compound patterns and irregular features systematically, but keeps them in proportion.

- It takes account of the shortcuts we take in everyday English speech.

- Its four principles cover all of the complications of English spelling.

Slimmed Down Spelling: key features

- **Sounds:** If we can hear a sound in a word, we need at least one letter for it. We need to listen very carefully, and sometimes to say words deliberately slowly, to make sure we don't miss any sounds.
- **Groups of letters:** We have only twenty-six letters, but several hundred thousand words in the English language. So, letters can't work on their own, but sometimes have to work in groups. We use a group of letters in a word when we know the word needs that group.
- **Extra letters:** Some words need to be spelled with a letter that does not represent a sound and is not part of a group. There is usually only one of these extra letters in a word. We only use an extra letter when we know the word needs it. If we only *think* the word needs it, we don't use it.
- **Awkward letters:** Sometimes the letter we need is not the one we think we need. We have to learn to make these variations with specific words.

> Taken together, these features give us two reasons for including a letter or group of letters in spelling a word — either we can hear the sound of the letter when we say the word (phonics), or we have learned that the word needs it. Essentially, we put together what we can hear and what we have learned.

Introducing Slimmed Down Spelling

It is best to introduce the approach as children learn to read in the Reception class and Year 1. All of the major schemes concentrate on the most regular patterns at the start, and it is straightforward to practise writing the words as children learn to read them. This should not be limited to writing them by hand – sets of plastic letters, for use on desktops and magnetic boards, are essential and invaluable tools for modelling spelling as they allow children to focus solely on the links between letters and sounds *without the additional demand of forming the letters by hand each time they spell a word.* This is particularly helpful to boys, whose motor control skills develop at a slower rate than girls, and who often form a negative view of themselves as a result of less neat handwriting. The more practice, games and modelling children receive in these early stages, the longer they have to establish these basic connections in their minds. This is crucial to later extension, and also to making things clear to the minority of children who have to work very hard to understand and use the patterns.

Once the sound category has been introduced, groups of letters, extra letters and awkward letters can be added as new patterns are taught in phonics lessons, and as children need to spell words in their writing. As with reading, this approach makes clear that sounds are the first and most important indicators of letters in spelling, but that children need to know other patterns as well. Explanation should be added at each stage, and in terms that make sense to the child, group or class. Children should never be made to do things they do not understand, and it is our job as teachers to make the explanations clear – this implies that they must not be more complicated than the phenomenon they seek to explain.

When I was at school in Glasgow in the 1950s, we were graded each day on our handwriting. Five out of five got you a star. Despite sweat and tears, I never got beyond two or three, until my mother persuaded my teacher to perjure herself by giving me a four. We now know that the cerebellum, located at the base of the brain near the spinal chord, develops more slowly in boys than in girls, and that this is a factor in boys' slower progress in handwriting. Nevertheless, many boys still equate handwriting with good work and intelligence. Separating handwriting from other aspects of literacy helps reduce stress and allows children to focus all of their attention on words and letters.

Try this: Clicker 5® for spelling

Clicker 5® is a software program that allows you to insert letters, words or phrases into cells in a grid on the lower half of a screen. Clicking on the letters or words lets you make words or sentences on a wordprocessor on the upper half of the screen. The program will read these back to you if you insert a full stop or right-click on a word. As you have control of the content, you can insert any single letters or groups that meet your class's needs, and load the program onto either a whiteboard or single computers. If you want to add further letters during a lesson, you can click on a keyboard (marked abc) and use any other letters you wish. Clicker 5® has won many awards, and your school may already have a copy in its ICT package. It can also be used to build sentences in foreign languages.

Set-up tip: If you use Clicker 5® for spelling, you will need to follow this series of clicks for each cell: select *Edit* (top toolbar), then *Edit mode*. Right-click on *Cell*. Click on *Properties*. Uncheck the box *Add space*; this ensures that the letters build words without spaces between them.

Bonus: Right-click on a letter after you have made your grid, and Clicker 5® will speak the letter name clearly.

Introducing Slimmed Down Spelling to older children and adults requires a different approach. These people have already met irregularity, and need the four aspects presented together so that they can see clearly how English spelling operates. I normally begin by explaining the following key points, which have been set out in previous chapters:

- We have twenty-six letters, and several hundred thousand words. Letters can't tell us all we need to know.

- We use what the letters tell us, but don't believe the letters tell us everything.

■ Most of the time letters represent sounds, and there is some link with sound in every word.

■ Our language is roughly 1,000 years old, and so has wrinkles.

Sounds

Explain that you will begin with some very simple words that they will almost certainly know already. I usually start by asking them to spell *cat*, with an apology for giving them such an elementary word, and say that in this word the letters tell us all we need to know. I will then add a few more regular three-letter words ending in *at*, just for practice. Children may write them on whiteboards so that you can check that everyone gets the idea. (In the rare cases in which children can't spell *cat*, I move to another regular -*at* word, such as *mat*, and play with it with plastic letters, having the child put the letters in the right order. I then change the first letter, and play with the new word. Once that is established, I switch the beginning letters and carry on until the consonant -*at* pattern is clearly established. Then I go back to *cat*, usually with success. (See Peter 's lesson in Chapter 2, page 18.)

Groups of letters

Next, introduce the idea of groups of letters. I do this by discussing team games, football or netball, where we work as a team, because we will lose if we try to win on our own. Our twenty-six letters have to make so many words that they sometimes need to work together in groups. Some groups are easy, as letters do what we expect, such as *sh*. It's worth discussing common groups with the class – *ch, sh, th, wh* – at this point. Have children write a lot of words with these two-letter groups, and note that the second letter in all of these is *h*.

Then, present the idea that some groups of letters do not produce the sound we expect. The best example to begin with is probably *tion* with simple words, such as *station* and *nation*, which have a single letter for each sound, and then the group. Explain that there are quite a lot of groups, and that we only use a group of letters when we've learned that the word needs it. Children can then be encouraged to find and note other words with *tion*. I would not introduce the alternative spellings at this stage – the idea is to establish that some words are spelled with single letter sounds, plus a group. Alternative groups require a further modification of thinking and are taught as they arise. Some of these groups come from foreign patterns, often French, but sometimes German; their origin and assimilation into English can usually be explained.

Extra letters

Having introduced sounds and groups, I move to extra letters, and explain that these do not give us a sound but usually help in other ways. This is true – most of them serve a purpose, and the best example to begin with is the final *e* – write the word *hat* on the board, and ask what letter would turn the word into *hate*. Practise with other words ending in *e* which have the same effect. (If you are using a scheme that presents the final e as part of a split digraph, you may prefer to begin with the next example.)

Double letters

Double letters are often used as a wall to keep the first vowel of a two-part word short – *hopping* rather than *hoping*, *shopping* rather than *sloping*, *slipping* rather than *sliding*. This does not form a rule, as some short vowels, such as rapid, come before a single consonant. It is, though, a useful pattern – two vowels separated by one consonant will often interact, with the first one representing a long sound. Some double letters, *l* and *s*, are found at the end of short words. The *s* makes the sound sharper – *less, Les* – but there is no clear reason for the *ll*. I teach children to look at words with *ll* and see how often it occurs at the end of a short word – any longer word has a single *l* at the end, giving us *careful, beautiful*.

Some other extra letters are used to form a wall, such as the *u* in *circuit* and *biscuit*, which stops the *i* from reaching the *c*. Other examples of these walls include the *u* in *plague, vague, vogue*.

Often extra letters are predictable: for example, the double *ll* at the end of a very short word, such as *ball, wall, tall*. There is often a pattern to them, such as the *mb* in *thumb, dumb, climb, plumber*.

Most words only have one extra letter, and we can usually find at least one other word that is like it. Each word then reinforces the other in the child's mind.

Tip

■ As with groups of letters, we only use an extra letter if we've learned that the word needs it. This helps avoid spelling errors of a type known as 'perseverance' – adding extra letters in the hope that more letters will make a word look more respectable. This is a surprisingly common error among less confident spellers.

Bonuses

■ Many words that appear very awkward to spell have only one point of difficulty. Chaos, for example, has one sound for each letter, with one extra letter, the *h*. It can be a real boost to the confidence of a weak speller to get this word right.
■ Very few words have more than one double letter; *accommodation, coffee, committee* are perhaps the most common, and these are not frequently used in primary school.

Awkward letters: usually vowels, but not always

As we have seen in Chapter 1, a vowel is not initially a letter but a sound made by the voice. The word originates in the French for voice, *voix*, which leads to a sound made by the voice, *voyelle*, the *y* changing to *w* in English. Our pronunciation of vowels is not always clear, and there have been changes over centuries that are not fully reflected in spelling. The letter we need to represent a vowel is therefore not always the one we think we need. For example, in *separate*, the middle *a* is not clearly pronounced and sounds more like *e*. We need to explain this phenomenon and to be ready for vowels not to work the way we expect. Fortunately, this difficulty usually only affects one letter in a word, and it is possible to link it to another word where the pronunciation is clearer. *Separate*, for example, can be linked with *parachute*. Both are from French, where there is no difference in the pronunciation. A good example to introduce the idea is *animal*, where the final vowel letter is pronounced as a clear, sharp *a* in French but slurred in English.

Most awkward letters are vowels, but *k* is also a problem. At the beginning of a word, it is used only as a strong letter, to prevent *c* being softened by *e*, *i* or *y*. At the end of a short word, it is used for the same sound as *c*, but only in a word of one syllable – *black*. But when do we use *k*, and when *ck*?

CASE STUDY

Difficulty with *k* or *ck*

Denis was ten and keen to do well. He spelled regular three-letter words accurately, but would always use *ck* at the end of a short word ending in a hard c sound. This was surprising, as Denis learned to use *c* on its own in longer words, such as *electric*. Denis's spelling worked for *brick*, but he would spell *bank* 'banck', even after several attempts. This upset him. We looked at a wide range of words ending in *k* – *make*, *book*, *link*, *lick*. A pattern that made sense to Denis was that the *k* always had at least one other letter with it – in a vowel group, such as look, beak or seek, the extra vowel letter kept it company. In *bank*, *n*, an extra consonant filled the function. In words that did not have any extra letter, *k* was reinforced by *c*, which did not change the sound.

Note: I can think of only two words, *trek* and *yak*, where *k* appears alone after a single vowel. These are recent introductions to English (first recorded usages 1795 and 1849 respectively), and I would explain this if Denis wanted to write these words. This seems unlikely before secondary school.

Snags, and how to deal with them

As teachers of spelling, our own knowledge and understanding of its strengths and weaknesses is a crucial resource. It enables us to explain to children why points of difficulty are as they are, and allows us to make the most of regular features to build confidence and keep irregularity in its place. This short section describes the most common problems and ways I have developed Slimmed Down Spelling to explain them to children, so that they know why they are having trouble, and how to get out of it. The solution is almost always to take the basic pattern and explain why there is a small twist to it, then develop a practical approach to each of the small variations. The analysis below is the basis of *Slimmed Down Spelling*. At all points in this process, vowels are crucial – there is more variation in vowel sounds than in consonants.

Saying the alphabet

When we say the alphabet, we add a vowel (voice) sound to each consonant letter – this sometimes leads us to think we 've put down all the letters we need, when we haven't.

We can't hear consonant sounds clearly when we pronounce them on their own – they need an element of voice to carry them through the air, or else they sound like a series of little clicks and other noises. Therefore, each consonant letter name in the alphabet has a voice, or vowel, element attached to it. The most common is the long or short sound of *e*, which appears in *b, c, d, e, f, g, l, m, n, p, s, t, v, x, z* – fifteen letters. Part of *a* appears in *a, h, j, k, r* – five letters. *Q* and *w* have part of *u*, and the remaining letters are vowels – if you prefer to consider *y* as a consonant, it has part of *i* in it.

Solution

Begin with an alphabet song with sounds rather than words. The 'Alphabet Song' (by Maureen Hartley, formerly deputy head of St Clare's School, Handsworth, Birmingham) begins as follows:

> Apple – a
> Apple – a, hanging on the tree
> (repeat)
> Bat – b
> Bat – b, see it hit my ball.

It proceeds through the alphabet in the same way, with a short word followed by the sound of the letter, *with no added voice sound*. It is straightforward to make up a similar song or ditty of your own. The accompanying CD gives words and tune of this version.

Maureen Hartley introduced letter names by making a rhyme with the names of children in the class, using 'Five, Six, Pick Up Sticks', for example:

> Anthony A, open the door
> Barbara B, sit on the floor

The exact rhyme varies with the names of the class, and imaginary ones can be invented if there are any letters missing. This is an ingenious idea, linking the children's own names with letter names, and it helps avoid confusion between names and sounds. The example here is reproduced on the accompanying CD.

Try this: explaining that a vowel is a voice sound

With the class very quiet, tell them that you are going to say a word, and then take a sound out of it. The word is a very simple one — *cat*. Now say *c-t*, taking the greatest care not to add any voice sounds to the two letters. Do this two or three times, encouraging the children to listen very closely. What have you left out? Most will tell you *a* or *ay*. Quite right. Now ask if they can hear your voice clearly when you've left the sound out. Repeat the *c-t* example, or make up some others with different letters. Children may not find it straightforward to identify the voice, but most can do so with practice, and this makes a good short session in a literacy lesson or starter. The activity builds children's understanding of the link between voice and vowel, which they can then use to distinguish between vowel and consonant.

Shortcuts and spelling

Shortcuts are socially neutral – we all take them when we speak, and none of us is allowed to take them when we write. However, the issue is not educationally neutral – the more shortcuts we take when we speak, the harder it is to bridge the gap between spoken and written English. Among the most frequent shortcuts in speech are:

- omitting *t* at the ends of words

- substituting *f* for *th*. To make *th*, we have to place our tongue between our teeth, and the shortcut involves touching the lips instead, with fewer movements of the mouth

- not pronouncing *h* in *when*, *which* and so on

- not pronouncing some vowel sounds clearly, particularly in the middle and at the ends of words. This is a strong characteristic of English – *animal* in French has the final *a* pronounced as clearly as the initial *a*. In English, the pronunciation of the final *a* is indistinct. The initial vowel sound in an English word is more likely to be clearly pronounced than a later one.

Solution

We need to explain shortcuts at the point of need. Not everyone takes the same shortcuts, and not every shortcut is unacceptable in Standard English. Nevertheless, the only opportunity some children have of speaking and learning the usage of formal English is in school, and teachers and teaching assistants need to provide both a model of accurate English and guidance in its use. Children may well need specific teaching to enable them to recognise and produce sounds such as *th* and *wh*, and all need practice in recognising vowel sounds that are not pronounced clearly enough to enable them to identify the letters they need. These issues and techniques need to be built into the scheme of work in a way that meets the needs of each individual school.

CASE STUDY

Simon and *when*, Michael and *uniform*

Simon was ten, and found it hard to know when to insert an *h* in words such as *when*. We began with *who*, which he pronounced with the back of his hand close to his lips, so he could feel his breath. We then discussed the late Fred Dibnah's pronunciation of *whole*, where he pronounced both *w* and *h*. In *who*, we agreed that we took a shortcut by leaving out *w*, and most of us take the same shortcut with *whole*. In *when*, *which* and *where*, many people leave out the *h* in everyday speech, leading to potential confusion with *went*, *witch* and *were*. We had to modify this speech pattern by taking care to include the *h*, again using the back-of-the-hand test. Simon did not find it easy, blowing too hard at times, but he understood, and gradually stopped making errors with these words.

Michael was nine, and interested in history. Writing about the differences between armies and unorganised hordes, he wrote that armies wore *uneform*. His mother and I agreed that neither of us could hear a distinct *i* in *uniform*, so we discussed with Michael other words with the same beginning – *unity*, *unify*, *universe*, *universal*. Once Michael could see the connection between the words, and the origin of uniform, he understood, and wrote uniform without difficulty.

Alphabet song

apple a, apple a, hanging on the tree

bat b, bat b, see it hit the ball

cat c, cat c, sitting on my lap

dog d, dog d, he can wag his tail

elephant e, elephant e, see her swing her trunk

fish f, fish f, swimming in the sea

gate g, gate g, close it when you go

hen h, hen h, see her with her chicks

insect i, insect i, crawling all around

jug j, jug j, for pouring out the milk

kite k, kite k, it can fly so high

lamb l, lamb l, with her woolly coat

mouse m, mouse m, running to his hole

nest n, nest n, a cosy home for birds

orange o, orange o, oh how good to eat!

purse p, purse p, keeps my money safe

queen q, queen q, sitting on her throne

rabbit r, rabbit r, with his floppy ears

seal s, seal s, diving in the sea

tiger t, tiger t, with a stripy back

umbrella u, umbrella u, we use it in the rain

van v, van v, driving up the road

window w, window w, we can see right through

box x, box x, hear it at the end

yawn y, yawn y, oh how tired we are!

zip z, zip z, for zipping up your coat

Class alphabet rhyme

_____ A closes the door.
_____ B sits on the floor.

_____ C picks up a book.
_____ D wants a look.

_____ E joins in as well.
_____ F has a tale to tell.

_____ G plays a game.
_____ H does the same.

_____ I is just looking, while
_____ J does the cooking.

_____ K feeds the fish, and
_____ L holds the dish.

_____ M plays with the sand.
_____ N holds up a hand.

_____ O goes out to play.
_____ P just runs away.

_____ Q stays in to help.
_____ R tidies the shelf.

_____ S is watching the screen.
_____ T shouts 'It's all gone green!'

_____ U is helping as well, when
_____ V hears the bell.

_____ W comes in from play.
_____ X has a lot to say.

_____ Y settles down again, with
_____ Z, who has the last name.

Photocopiable: *Using Phonics to Teach Reading and Spelling*
Paul Chapman Publishing © John Bald 2007

One sound, several spellings

We sometimes have several choices of spelling to represent a sound. This problem can affect both vowels and consonants.

Consonants

The sound *c*, as in *cat*, can be made with *c, k, ck* or *que – cat, kill, stick, unique.*

C and *g* may be softened by *e, i* or *y* to produce a sound close to that of *s* or *j –
cell, city, cycle, gem, gin, Egypt.*

Sh, as in *ship*, can be represented in various ways towards the end of longer
words – *station, possession, occasion, social, confidential.* There are slight variations
in this pronunciation, but the sounds are very similar.

Vowels

A vowel is, first and foremost, a sound made by the voice, and not the letter or
group of letters that represents it. Estimates of the number of voice sounds in
English are usually in the mid-twenties, and we have only seven letters with
which to write them – *a, e, i, o, u, w* and *y.* The last two are variations on *u* and
i, which can be heard when we say the names of *y* and *w.*

Terminology: long and short vowel sounds, vowel groups, diphthongs

A *long* vowel sound can be described fairly accurately as the name of a letter, as in
the examples *made, mere, Mike, more, mute.*

A *short* vowel sound is the most common sound represented by each of these vowels
– *mad, met, mit, mock, mud.*

In some schemes, using *e* at the end of a word to make the preceding vowel 'say
its name' is referred to as a *split digraph.* That is, the group of two letters that
represents one voice sound is 'split ' by one – and, rarely, by more than one –
consonant. This terminology links the final *e* to other vowel groups, but
requires the children to learn the term *digraph.* My alternative is to consider the
final *e* as giving information that changes the sound of the first vowel. This

avoids young children having to learn linguistic terminology, and introduces the idea of one letter providing information about another, which helps later in dealing with soft *c* and *g*. There is no evidence on this point, though, and it is a matter of professional judgement.

A *diphthong* is a compound of two different voice sounds. To make them, we move the muscles of our mouth and our tongue as we pronounce the sound. To say *oi*, for example, we begin with our tongue at the bottom of our mouth for the *o*, and then raise it and move it backwards. We are rarely conscious of doing this, so try it. To say *cow*, we first open and then close our mouth as we produce the sound. These compound vowels are more frequent in English than in Spanish or Italian, though they do occur in German. They are sometimes known as *glides*, to reflect the smooth changing of the sound as it is said.

Alternative spellings of long vowel sounds:

ai, ay and *a* with *a-e*: *maid, may, make*

ee, ea, e-e: *bee, Beatrice, here*

ie, igh and *y*: *pie, night, my, bite*

ow, oe, o-e: *slow, toe, note*

u, u-e: *usual, use.*

There are fewer variations in the spelling of short vowel sounds, but the following are the most common:

e, ea: *bed, dead*

i, y : *ship, any*

u, o: *dud, come, mother.*

Dipthongs:

oi, oy : *boil, boy*

ou, ow: *shout, cow*

eu, ew: *Europe, few.*

Solutions

Children need to build up a mental picture of these groups over time, and with the aid of explanation and practice. Apart from the very unusual pattern *ough*, which is considered below, this is the most difficult area of spelling, and vowel groups have been identified as a particular weakness in national testing for 11-year-olds. This teaching therefore needs to continue throughout the primary school. However, patterns in the examples above show that vowel spelling is not just a random process. We do not like English words to end in *u* or *i*, for example, so we tend to have *y* or *w* at the end of words, and *i* or *u* in the middle (a similar dislike applies to *v*, which we tackle by adding *e* to words such as *have, love, give*). We can organise practice by grouping words with the same spelling together, and by encouraging children to keep a personal notebook in which they build up their own collection of words, and always find at least one word that is like any they have just learned to spell.

Groups of letters representing different sounds

Some groups of letters can represent several different sounds. This is less frequent than alternative spellings for the same sound. There are two main examples, the vowel group *ea*, and *ough*, which is the most awkward group in the whole language.

Ea represents both the short and long sounds of *e*, and a range of other sounds. Some of most common examples are listed below. The explanation I give to children is that this group of letters is overworked, but that they can remember the words in groups. When they are reading, if a word does not make sense I suggest they try one of the alternative voice sounds to see if that words better. In order to read and spell words with this group, a child or adult needs to adjust their thinking to select from a variety of possibilities – this is a prime example of using what the letters tell us, without believing that they tell us everything. The learning can be reinforced by games and quizzes.

head	sea
dead	tea
bead	tease
instead	please

sound　　　　　　　　　　　name

awkward

bear

pear

tear

wear

steak

break

Ough spellings

According to the *Oxford Companion to the English Language*, *ough* spellings were regularised by printers towards the end of the seventeenth century. They are the most irregular and variable in their sound correspondence in the language, but can be cut down to size provided that the letter combination is thoroughly memorised, by fair means or foul: saying it over and over again, and then writing it several times, covering each version before beginning the next, mixing up plastic letters and putting them in the right order, and anything else that comes to mind. Next, the irregularities themselves can be grouped together, leaving only *through* to be taught on its own, normally with some examples showing it in context.

Word groupings with *ough*:

ought	rough	plough	thorough
bought	tough	bough	borough
thought	enough	Slough	
brought			
sought		trough	dough
wrought		cough	though
fought			although

Some sentences for *through*:

No through road.

I'm through with this.

He went straight through a red light.

You might also like to teach this word with a humorous picture.

Some more extra letters

Silent letters at the beginning, and sometimes the end, of a word are usually the result of a change in pronunciation – the sound represented has been dropped, and the letter remains. There is usually a pattern to these words, which helps greatly with learning them. Silent *k* at the beginning of a word is always followed by *n* (*knight, know, knob*), and silent *w* by *r* (*wrist, write, wrong*). A silent *b* at the end of a word is preceded by *m* (*climb, plumb, lamb*). A set of blank playing cards can be used to make a snap game for these words.

FURTHER READING

There is little research in synthetic phonics and English spelling, but students may care to explore the selection and categorisation of spelling groups in *Alpha to Omega* (Hornsby 1999), recommended in Chapter 4.

Phonics and more advanced literacy skills

This chapter will:

■ Consider the demands made by advanced literacy, and how to plan for them in the curriculum

■ Describe regular and irregular features in more advanced vocabulary

■ Show how phonics operate in words with several syllables

Beyond the infant school, the texts children read often challenge them in several areas at the same time. These include:

■ Texts become longer; most have fewer illustrations, but there may be more diagrams.

■ Sentences become more varied, and many become removed from the structures of everyday speech.

■ Vocabulary becomes more varied, with a growing proportion of words derived from Latin and Greek.

■ The information conveyed in texts becomes more complex, and harder to understand at a literal level.

■ Children are required to attend to meanings which are not explicitly stated in the text.

■ Print becomes smaller.

The role of phonics within this complex picture needs to be carefully defined. Phonics do not develop children's vocabulary unless they are accompanied by careful attention to the detailed meaning of the words, including words with similar phonic structures, and the text, which provides context. Rose's (1986:70) recommendation of a language-rich context is as relevant in junior and secondary schools as in the early stages of reading. This means that opportunities for structured discussion need to be planned as a normal part of teaching in all subjects, and that teachers need to take time to explain new words so that children understand them. This is particularly important for children whose experience of formal language is limited to what they hear in school.

CASE STUDY

Gateway Primary School

Most children join Gateway Primary School with little or no knowledge of English. After systematic phonics teaching in the infant school, reading, writing, speaking and listening are systematically built into policies for all subjects in Years 3 to 6. As a result, pupils' skills are very consistently developed, and overall standards are above national average standards in English, mathematics and science by the age of eleven. Gateway Primary School was *Evening Standard* London School of the Year in 2006. The following example is from its Ofsted report (2005).

An excellent lesson in Year 5 enabled pupils to develop very clear understanding of events leading to the foundation of the Anglican church.

Pupils showed excellent understanding and recall of their earlier learning about Tudors in the starter session. Well-known portraits of the main characters were then enlarged on the interactive whiteboard, described, and their roles discussed. In exploratory talk, using key questions, the teacher focused attention on these characters, and asked pupils for a) the feelings, and b) persuasive arguments, stemming from them, relating to Catherine of Aragon and Henry VIII. These were recorded on illustrated prints from the interactive whiteboard, then discussed.

The teacher then modelled the process to be worked on using another character. In groups of three, pupils worked collaboratively as reader, recorder and reporter, using sources, making notes, and reporting back to class for evaluation. Their grids showed an excellent grasp of how personal feelings led to national events. The teaching was lively and informed throughout, enthusing pupils with a zest for knowledge.

▶

In the final session, the teacher summed up, outlining later events, culminating with the situation of the monarchy in Britain today, appointing bishops on the advice of the Prime Minister. The very high quality of written work and presentation in this lesson was reflected in very attractive classroom displays of work in history and geography.

Recurring phonic patterns: 'soft' *c* and *g*

Among the most important additions to basic phonics is the softening effect of *e*, *i* or *y* after *c* and *g*. This requires a significant adjustment to the thinking involved in basic phonic processing. Children will have met the first of these, typically at the ends of words such as *face*, *place*, *page*, in the early stages of learning to read, but the patterns become more frequent in junior and secondary school at the beginning of words.

Virtually always, except in a few words derived from Welsh, *e*, *i*, or *y* will soften the sound of *c*. *Cent*, and words including it, is perhaps the most frequent example, as it occurs in the metric system and in history. *Ci* is also very frequent – *city*, *circle*. *Cy* is less common, but important words such as *cycle*, *emergency*, make it significant.

The same three letters produce a similar effect on *g* – *general*, *gin*, *energy*. There are, though, three very common words, *girl*, *get* and *give*, where it does not operate. The pattern should therefore be presented as one that works most of the time.

Try This: Softening *c* or *g*

As soon as the children are ready for it, and at the latest towards the beginning of Year 3, introduce the concept of softening *c* or *g* in a specific lesson. Explain that the effect comes from Latin and French words that have come into English, and that it is quite straightforward once they have got the idea that some letters change the sounds made by other letters. You might use the following lists of words, breaking them down slowly into their sounds, and having the children read them with you. Add or substitute words to suit your class.

centre	city	mercy
cell	civilian	cycle
cent	circle	bicycle
innocent	circus	cygnet
recent	recipe	Cyprus
century	cider	
necessary	science	
gem	gin	energy
general	gipsy	gyrate
generous	Gillian	Egypt
gene	vigil	clergy
gestation		edgy
digest		
congestion		
edge		

Follow up by having children practise in groups, and then use games and quizzes for reinforcement. Enter the words in the children's personal word books, and have them find other words with the same pattern. Making this pattern a focus for up to a term's work should firmly establish the pattern for all pupils.

Advanced phonics: Latin

As children move through the primary school, they increasingly meet words of Latin and Greek origin. These use a system of basic words, known as roots, combined with prefixes and suffixes that enable each root word to be used in a variety of ways. These small additions are phonically regular, and have the effect of putting a multiplier on vocabulary – once the technique is mastered, it is difficult to learn a word without learning another.

This curious word shows how regular prefixes and suffixes can be used to build layers of meaning. In addition to *ed*, *ly* and *ing*, which children will have met, the most common prefixes and suffixes include:

un	*pre*
dis	*ante*
de	*inter*

anti	*mid*
counter	*post*
re	*over*
ment	*under*

A Victorian example

To *establish* something is to set it up. In the Church of England, adding *ment* to make *establishment*, had the particular meaning of incorporating the Church as part of the state, an arrangement that allowed it to levy taxes, or tithes. Someone who was against this system would advocate *disestablishment*, and adding another suffix allows him or her to be described as a *disestablishmentarian*. Those who reacted against this added the prefix *anti*, and were *antidisestablishmentarians*. Their cause added *ism*, much like *communism*, and became *antidisestablishmentarianism*.

Add these to a range of common root words, and you have the basis of an adult vocabulary. The process can be compared to linguistic building blocks – you just have to make sure your prefix fits the connection. In order to use this system fluently, children need to practise words with similar patterns, meet them in texts they read and use them in their writing in order to understand what the letters are telling them in each context. The idea can be presented in a similar unit to that set out above for soft *c* and *g*, and would also make a good focal point for perhaps over a term.

Advanced phonics: Greek

The most common patterns taken from Greek are substitutions rather than new patterns – *ch* for *k*, *ph* for *f*, *y* for *i* near the beginning of a word. These can also be the basis for a unit, though perhaps from Year 4 onwards. The following are common examples, and it is perhaps best to stick to very common words at first, and to note others as they arise in children's work. Greek is also the source of a silent *p* at the beginning of some technical words.

chaos	elephant	physical
chemist	photo	physics
ache	photograph	psychology
stomach	photographer	
choir	photographic	
chronicle	philosophy	
chronic		

Teaching children to read words with several syllables

An easy starting point is to clap the word, and have the children say and clap it with you. Each clap will naturally fall in with a vowel, and so represent the syllable, and you can then return and explain the link between the syllables and the vowel sounds. Some children will learn polysyllabic words at home, and others will not. It is therefore important to pick them out and practise them at school, and to have children develop the habit of finding another word that is like the one they have just learned. Keeping personal word lists, and taking time to discuss the meaning of longer words, are also essential to understanding as well as to memory.

FURTHER READING

The Reading Crisis: Why Poor Children Fall Behind, Chall et al. (1990) Cambridge, MA: Harvard University Press. An important piece of research showing the effects of the increasing demands of literacy on transfer to secondary school on patterns of reading. The chief finding was that the gap between children of highly educated parents and those from working class families became much greater in the early years of secondary school. The main reason for this was that the former were able to adapt much more readily to the demands of texts that were not expressed in everyday language.

Reading for Learning in the Sciences and *Learning from the Written Word*, Eric Lunzer and Keith Gardner (1984). Edinburgh: Oliver and Boyd for the Schools Council. Two books from a reading project that provided useful examples of reading activities in the context of lessons in a wide range of subjects.

CHAPTER 7

Resources

This chapter will:

■ Propose a strategy for building a phonics resources bank
■ Review core phonics schemes and other phonics resources
■ Consider additional resources that can contribute to phonic work

Resources for teaching phonics fall into four main categories:

■ **Core schemes**: A core scheme contains activities that take children from the initial stages of phonic work to the point at which they have sufficient knowledge and skills to read independently. Core schemes vary in their scope: some cover the whole of the first three years in primary school, with extension materials for older children, while others are limited to the very early stages of learning to read. Selecting the core scheme is a crucial decision, as the whole school will have to use it. The core scheme's handbook or guidance notes should form the basis of a scheme of work, and may even make this unnecessary.

■ **Supplementary resources**: These reinforce or extend the core scheme, and are a smaller-scale purchase. They may be ICT- or book-based.

■ **Courses and materials for special educational needs**: The best of these offer smaller steps, clear explanation and additional support. The worst are a grind, focusing all of a child's attention on one phonic pattern in isolation, with no attention to the application of phonic skills in reading text. These risk becoming an alternative curriculum, which does not allow work to be reinforced in normal lessons. Rose (2006: 42) is right to point out that special lessons are not a substitute for effective teaching in class.

■ **Books and resources for teachers and teaching assistants**: A school's most important resource is the knowledge, skills and understanding of its staff. As a minimum, teachers and teaching assistants need to read the handbooks of schemes so that they understand what the resources are trying to achieve. Further reading is seldom wasted, and everyone should be encouraged to read beyond the immediate demands of their training courses. Such reading encourages evaluation and independent judgement.

Core schemes

The various core schemes are reviewed below, giving first the publication, materials or product details.

Fast Phonics First, Joyce Watson and Rhona Johnston. www.heinemann.co.uk, primary. Teachers' Guide, plus 5 CDs, also available online.

The materials developed as the basis of the authors' research in Clackmannanshire comprise a sixteen-week course, to be taught in class sessions of 20–30 minutes per day, with an additional ten minutes for individual or group work. This revised Whiteboard version is attractively presented and easy to use, with the scheme of work built into the software, and full plans for each daily lesson in the *Teaching Guide*. The *Teaching Guide* is a model of clarity and compactness, and will save users much unnecessary work. The main additional resource needed is magnetic boards and letters, which the authors suggest should be provided one between two children, so that they can discuss their work and explain to each other what they are doing and why.

Teaching is based on the teacher modelling and rehearsing work with the whole class. Teachers discuss the purpose of each lesson at the beginning, and what has been learned at the end. There is an alphabet song, and letter sounds are introduced at a rate of one sound per day. They are grouped into thirteen units, with a round-up 'language session' at the end of each unit. Children learn the difference between letter names and sounds from the beginning. Irregular words are fed into the scheme after the regular elements of these words have been introduced, but the reasons why these words are irregular are not explained. The whiteboard graphics include a friendly animal to provide encouragement, and there is an easily accessible selection of games to reinforce perception of sounds, letter names, reading and spelling. A 'magnetic board' feature allows letters to be combined on the whiteboard in the same way they would be on a small board, and shared with the class. The scheme of work and this feature make it straightforward for teachers to teach spelling alongside reading.

The scheme does not use books for the first six units, where the language-rich element of teaching is provided by means of books and stories read by the teacher. After this point, the authors suggest introducing a graded scheme. The idea is to introduce books when children have enough knowledge to be able to apply it in reading, and some familiarity with irregular words. The authors recommend that books be carefully chosen, and that teachers should help children anticipate difficulties. Schools in the original research used *Jolly Phonics* (see below) for graded reading, but *Read, Write Inc.* (also below) provides an alternative. Terminology is formal, but limited to six terms: *blend*, *cluster*, *digraph*, *phoneme*, *grapheme* and *segment*. Teachers taking part in the Clackmannanshire research had high praise for this scheme; 'best for thirty years' was a typical comment, and their views were confirmed by the visits of Rose (2006: 61–5) and his team to their schools.

Core Scheme Summary: *Fast Phonics First*

Pros:
Very clear design, accessible, easy to use for teachers and children.
Excellent Handbook, incorporating well-designed scheme of work.
Excellent whiteboard presentation and games.
Teaches spelling alongside reading.
Cons:
Covers only the first sixteen weeks of teaching.
Does not explain why some words are irregular.
Does not have its own graded reading books.
Conclusion:
Highly recommended. The whiteboard transfer is very successful, and the *Teaching Guide* is a major strength. The overall approach has been tried and tested more systematically than any other. This is, however, a sixteen-week course, and schools therefore need to plan carefully for what will follow it.

Jolly Phonics, Sue Lloyd and others, www.jollylearning.co.uk. This teaching pack includes: *The Phonics Handbook, Jolly Phonics Wordbook, Jolly Phonics video, Finger Phonics, Finger Phonics Big Books, Jolly Phonics Wall Freize, Cards, Letter Sound Strips, Jolly Jingles, Spelling and Alphabet posters, Tricky Word Wallflowers.*

Jolly Phonics grew out of the author's work at Woods Loke School in Suffolk, which consistently achieved better reading results than comparable local schools. It is used successfully in many schools, including Gateway Primary School, the *Evening Standard* London School of the Year for 2006. It divides phonic teaching into five basic skills:

1. Learning the letter sounds.

2. Learning letter formation.

3. Blending – for reading.

4. Identifying the sounds in words – for writing .

5. Tricky words – irregular words.

Letters are introduced at a rate of one a day over the first four weeks, with two-letter combinations – *ai, oa, ie, ee, or, ng, oo, ch, sh, teach, qu, ou, oi, ue, er, ar* – introduced from week four onwards. The Handbook is clearly written, with a straightforward outline plan and explanations of the teaching methods. There is a simple story to introduce each letter, with good, large actions that help reinforce its shape, and a photocopiable master which can be coloured – good reinforcement of pencil control at this stage – with lines to practise letter formation underneath. Children learn to write their name in week 2, and begin to work with tricky words from week 6 onwards, though they do not have an explanation of why words are tricky. Some of the spelling techniques are also questionable, particularly the look–copy–cover–write check approach. This is less flexible than the magnetic boards used by *Fast Phonics First*, and the movement of the eyes back and forward while copying distracts attention from combining the letters to form words. Gateway School made its own whiteboard materials to support the lessons, and teaching assistants work with groups of children in each lesson to ensure that everyone understands and joins in. This led to several cameos for excellence in its Ofsted inspection report.

The Handbook has a good selection of additional activities on photocopy masters, and similar activities are provided in a series of workbooks. The accompanying 'Finger Phonics' are produced in big books and in card books, which ingeniously provide a template for children to finger-trace letters and groups of letters by cutting their shapes into the double thickness of the card. These are colourful books, with small groups of words with similar spelling on each page. There is a series of graded readers, which are brightly presented but with rather tame storylines. They do, though, have words listed on the back cover in ways that provide a good format for practice. The additional resources provide valuable and consistent reinforcement.

Core Scheme Summary: *Jolly Phonics*

Pros:

Well organised, with clear progression and a well-written Handbook.

Good, large actions that help children remember letter formation.

Good introduction of letter formation through Finger Phonics.

Attractive big books.

Cons:

Weak storylines in some of the graded readers.

Does not explain *why* some words are tricky.

Conclusion:

This scheme has important strengths, and plays an important part in the work of many successful schools. It should be considered carefully alongside the other core schemes to determine which meet a school's needs best. Elements, particularly Finger Phonics, may be useful alongside other schemes.

Read, Write Inc. Ruth Miskin www.oup.co.uk

Ruth Miskin developed her approach when she was headteacher of Kobi Nazrul School in East London, which has a very high proportion of children with English as an additional language. The acknowledged success of this school was based on several innovations, including new techniques for managing classes, an extension of the role of the teaching assistant, and organisation to provide support to children as soon as they needed it. The resulting combination of clear teaching techniques and management information make these materials unique, and they have been continuously updated following feedback from training course participants, colleagues and HMI. They give practitioners the means to take children from the initial stages of reading to the point at which they can read independently, with enjoyment and understanding at levels beyond the literal meaning of words. This makes them a unique resource.

The scheme presents a total of forty sounds, sensibly described throughout as 'sounds' rather than 'phonemes', though it retains 'grapheme', as the author thinks this is simpler than referring to 'a letter or a group of letters'. Following the success of *Fast Phonics First*'s use of magnetic letters for early spelling, it offers its own set, which is compact enough for children to take home on a backing card. At an early stage, children learn to use 'Fred Talk'. Fred is a character who can only speak in words of one syllable, and has to break each word down into its sounds, without adding extra voice sounds. This is an effective technique, which teachers can return to at any point in the day to reinforce children's perceptions of sound. There is a complete plan for each lesson, integrating work with cards, a well-designed whiteboard presentation and letter formation.

As soon as sounds and words are taught, there are additional activities to speed up children's recognition of sounds, so that word identification becomes so quick that children can begin to phrase their reading naturally. As children do not have the skills to read books independently from the outset, the early texts are 'ditty' sheets, which children first read and then illustrate to show that they have understood them. Although these sheets are not books, they are designed to be meaningful to the children using them, for example:

hot chips from the shop
a can of pop from the shop
hot chips and pop
mmmm

The message is not nutritionally correct, but the text can be imbued with energy and enthusiasm, and in fact contains more words than the early books of some reading schemes.

Children are not expected to read all of these ditties – they move on to storybooks once they can read some of them easily. The storybooks are amusing, attractively illustrated with dotty cartoon characters, and contain significant innovations, the most important being the emphasis on questions and discussion that is systematically built into each book. Some questions at each stage can be answered by detailed reference to the text, and others encourage children to think about why people do things, and how they feel. Questions and complete instructions are printed on the inside cover of each book, so that parents can use the same approach as the school when reading with children at home. Words are printed on the inside back cover to be used for more speeding-up activities. There are seventy-five storybooks, divided into seven levels, so that there is plenty of practice at each level. The books are a major resource in their own right. A series of 'Get Writing' books, introduced at the same time as the storybooks, enables children to hold sentences in their head and write them, as well as composing their own.

Throughout the scheme, words are grouped in two categories: green, phonically regular and red, irregular. In the early stages, a few regular words are listed as 'temporarily red' as they contain phonic patterns that have not yet been taught. The author's training sessions give the children an everyday explanation of why words are not always regular, but this is not contained in the Handbook. There seems no clear reason for the omission – a child reading a book does not know whether any unknown word is 'green' or 'red', and the lack of guidance on tackling irregularity is the scheme's only weakness.

The social dimensions of the classroom are considered in more depth than in any other resource, and contain further innovations. To promote the involvement of all children, each has a working partner, and the guidance on training children to work in partnership is outstandingly clear and practical. Issues such as grouping children according to their learning needs, tracking progress, introducing and managing support – any child falling behind receives an immediate booster course of 10- to 15-minute lessons with a teacher or teaching assistant in the afternoon – are described in such detail that virtually any school will find useful ideas, whether or not they buy into the whole scheme. Ruth Miskin says the work requires 'passion and relentlessness', and this comes through in every word and every moment of her training course.

Core Scheme Summary: *Read, Write Inc.*

Pros:

■ Excellent Handbook, with detailed guidance on management and teaching.

■ Attractive, funny books develop understanding alongside phonics.

■ Excellent organisation of additional support.

■ Very clear planning for each lesson.

■ A very useful range of specific techniques, including 'Fred Talk'.

■ All children are involved and included.

■ Outstanding track record in schools in disadvantaged areas.

■ Very well designed training courses.

Cons:

Not enough guidance on explaining irregularity in the hamdbook.

Conclusion:

My first choice for a core scheme. Its scope and detailed description of effective teaching and management techniques are unmatched by the other materials, and the reading books are a major innovation at infant level. It does, however, require clarity and commitment on the part of all staff, and schools introducing it can expect to meet this in their training.

Supplementary resources

■ **Oxford Reading Tree, Woodpeckers**: This short series of books from the middle range of the scheme is phonically based, with well illustrated stories that children have found interesting, though they don't always have the same appeal to adults. I have used it successfully with weak readers in junior schools.

■ **An interactive whiteboard**: This provides a dimension of involvement and movement that helps hold young children's attention and enhances learning. It is most helpful to be able to move text around the screen like clay on a potter's wheel, and to watch children's eyes as they follow letters being combined to make words. The effect that can be gain in individual work with a pack of plastic letters is enhanced for a class through the use of the whiteboard, and teachers should have access to this technology, and training in its use, wherever possible.

CASE STUDY

Whiteboards and learning at Gateway Primary School

Gateway Primary School has over 90 per cent of pupils learning English as an additional language. It won the *Evening Standard* London School of the Year Award in 2006. Headteacher Keith Duggan gave priority to the installation of whiteboards in each classroom, and invested heavily on training for each teacher to use them confidently and well. Lessons across the school reflected this, as teachers had the skills to design and adapt their own resources to the whiteboard. A particularly successful example was a series of activities based on *Jolly Phonics*, in which children would combine letters and groups of letters on the screen to make the words they were learning in their books. Grouping words according to their sounds was used to reinforce set theory in maths. The sound start in early reading made an important contribution to outstanding results in national tests for 11-year-olds, with a particularly high proportion reaching Level 5.

- **Supporting books**: Although some schemes do not use books in the beginning stages of reading, it is not necessary to exclude books that include irregular words, provided children understand from the beginning that phonics works most, but not all of the time. Once they are used to the idea that phonics are a help rather than a complete solution to identifying words, even lower-attaining children become used to the idea that they will not be able to work out all words from phonics, and are much less frightened to try words out as a result. To provide variety and sustain interest, each school needs a collection of books that it finds helpful to children of a wide range of abilities, and to encourage the children to read them. Some of these may be books at a similar level from a range of reading schemes, and others will be children's storybooks, sometimes described as 'real books', which should be in the library as well as classrooms. The key professional skill lies in knowing the books and picking out those which will help and interest each child. Ruth Miskin put it well when she said, in response to a question on BBC2's *Newsnight*, 'The only point of learning phonics is to read a book.'

■ **Synthetic Phonix**: (Sue Palmer, www.philipandtacey.co.uk) Two bags of coloured, interlocking cubes, some with single letters, others with letter groups. The cubes fit together to make words. Children can then either keep their words, or substitute letters to make other words with similar patterns. The second bag introduces two- and three-letter blends, and requires the single letters from the first to make words. A colourful and simple resource for young children.

■ **Language Master**: (www.drakeed.co.uk) Language Master reads words or sentences from a strip of tape at the bottom of a card. The tape has two tracks, one for the teacher and one for the child, so that the child can hear the teacher read a word, then say it themselves and compare the two versions. At the same time, the teacher has a record of a child's exact reading of a word, which may help focus attention on specific aspects of speech that need development. Cards come in various sizes, and blank cards are particularly useful, as they allow supporting material and illustrations to be added to words. Teachers can build up sets of words for particular purposes, and have them available to children for practice. The machines can be used with headphones, and are also helpful for small group work. Language Master is not new technology, but its versatility has not always been fully exploited. It is equally useful for teaching English as an additional language. When Georgia Lewis, Deputy Head of Rushmore School in Hackney, took the school's Language Master on a teaching visit to in South Africa, the twinned school asked for six machines to be shipped out to them.

■ **Blank Playing Cards**: (www.spiritgames.co.uk) Blank cards are available at £1.99 per 100. Very useful for making resources and games with a professional look.

■ **Games from the CD**: The accompanying CD contains a number of games which can provide extra practice in making and remembering words. These are: Snakes and Ladders, Snakes and Ladders First Words, Long Snake Race Game, three sets of word jigsaws, Phonics Bank and Final E Grid. The blank formats can, of course, be used as you please, though I try to avoid placing very similar words in adjacent squares.

Resources for special educational needs

■ *Nessy*: (www.nessy.co.uk) A series of phonic games designed to speed up word recognition. Originally designed for children who had been assessed as dyslexic, Nessy has a genuinely interesting selection of reading and spelling games at seven levels, with an option for teachers to make their own games. Games can be played at various speeds, and even adults have to have their wits about them as the games speed up. Recommended for use as specific reinforcement; with careful planning, this resource can provide support for weaker primary readers of any age.

■ *Wordshark*: (www.rm.com) A simpler format than *Nessy*, but with similar qualities. The basic benefit of these programs is in speeding up skills that have been taught, and this one also needs to be carefully targeted. *Wordshark* is a compilation of games that provides useful practice for word recognition. The games are brightly coloured and popular with children. They can be played at various speeds, and there is a good reward system. Provided the games are carefully selected, *Wordshark* makes a valuable addition to a school's resources.

Snakes and ladders

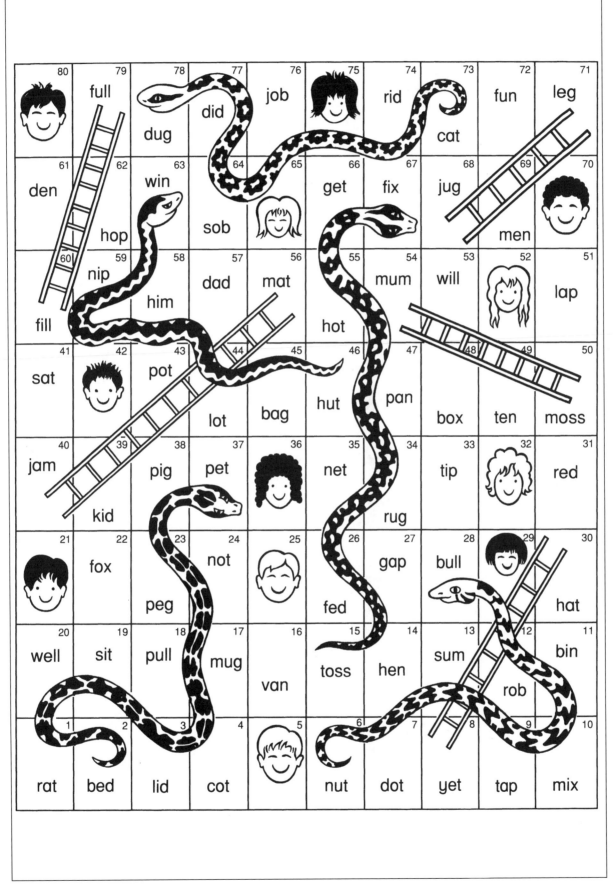

Snakes and ladders first words

Long snake race game

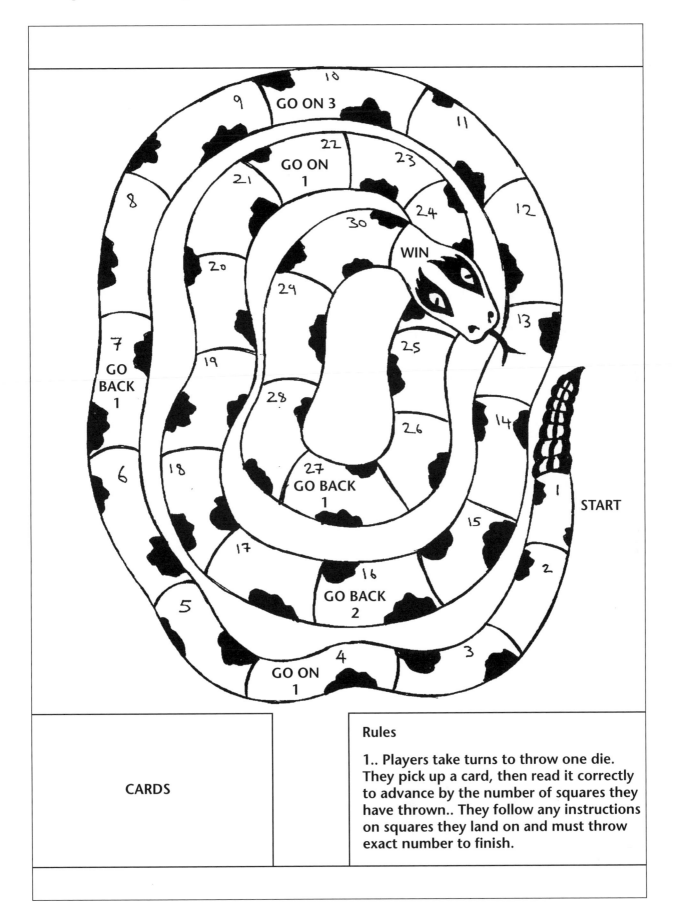

Rules

1.. Players take turns to throw one die. They pick up a card, then read it correctly to advance by the number of squares they have thrown.. They follow any instructions on squares they land on and must throw exact number to finish.

CARDS

Word jigsaw 1

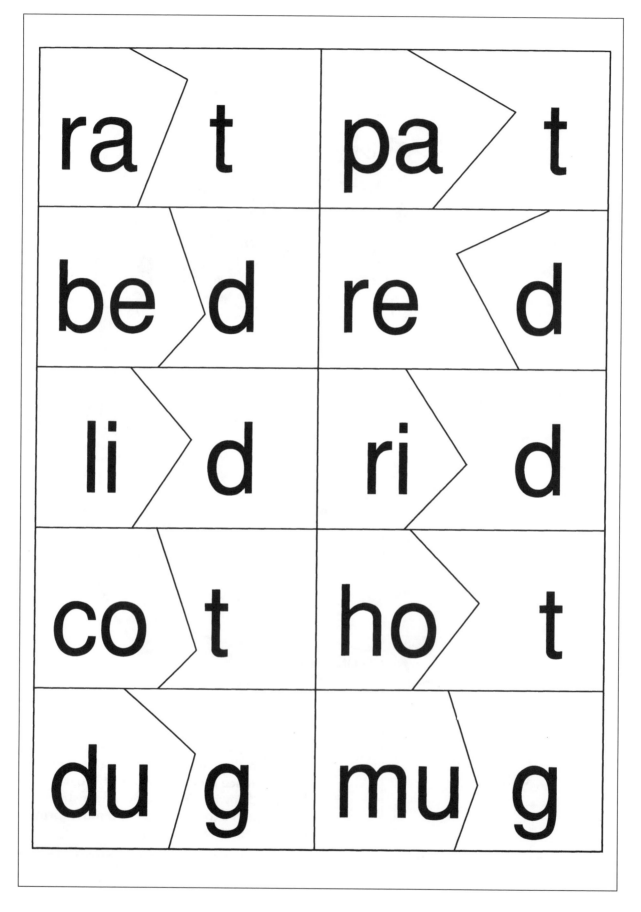

ra t   pa t

be d   re d

li d   ri d

co t   ho t

du g   mu g

Word jigsaw 2– blank

Word jigsaw 3 – blank

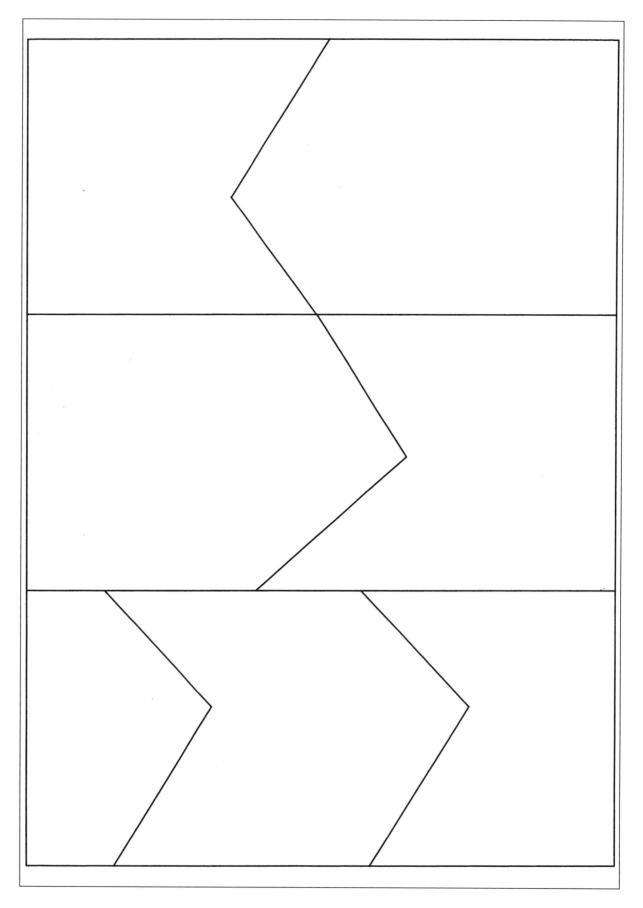

Final E grid

	A	B	C	D	E
1	hate	late	date	care	fare
2	here	these	pipe	ride	line
3	pole	bore	more	rope	dope
4	use	fuse	tune	cute	cure
5	slate	plate	scare	stare	stake
6	Drake	flake	take	make	bake
7	cake	mistake	sake	whale	gale
8	tale	tripe	ripe	stripe	wipe
9	polite	smile	pile	tile	mile
10	while	white	bite	whine	pine
11	spine	shine	mine	hire	nice
12	spice	twice	mice	rice	dice
13	rake	fake	fluke	Duke	Luke
14	hate	plate	inflate	complete	snore
15	score	deplore	fire	wire	inspire
16	hire	wine	like	bike	Mike
17	create	nine	time	tame	game
18	same	lame	name	blame	prime
19	twine	daze	graze	maze	amaze
20	fine	refine	delete	Crete	amuse
21	refuse	confuse	ruse	state	price
22	salute	guide	inside	wide	pride
23	dome	Rome	home	Clive	alive
24	drive	strive	wife	knife	strife

■ *Alpha to Omega*: (Bevé Hornsby, www.heinemann.co.uk) This is a pioneering work of analysis of English spelling, originally designed for use in a dyslexia clinic in a London hospital. It consists of groups of words with similar spellings, followed by a series of dictations. The dictations can easily become a grind, and I very rarely use them, but the word-lists are compiled with great care. I found them very helpful in my early years as a literacy teacher, and recommend them as a quick way of finding word families, including some of the less obvious ones.

FURTHER READING

The Handbook to *Read, Write Inc.* should be read by all co-ordinators, whether or not they use the scheme, for its guidance on organisation and management.

CHAPTER 8

What Additional Techniques Can Help the Weakest Readers?

This chapter will:

■ Describe assessment techniques, based on direct observation

■ Consider the effects of hearing difficulty, and of sensitivity to light

■ Show how to adapt teaching to tackle reading and spelling difficulties

■ Show how to sustain interest and identify progress

■ Consider the contribution of assistants, parents and carers

■ Show how effective teaching can be built on in the course of normal lessons

■ Show how planning for individual needs can be built into a school's systems

We know in advance that, in any group of children, there will be some that will find literacy more difficult than others. We also know what these children's problems are likely to be, and what approaches can be used to tackle them. It makes sense, therefore, to plan in advance to deal with these difficulties as soon as they arise, so that as many children as possible will be able to learn happily and well, first time. As children progress in reading, however, they find that texts get longer and print tends to get smaller. This can lead to some difficulties that are not present in the initial stages, and this implies that monitoring of progress needs to be a permanent feature.

To help a child who is struggling with any aspect of reading or writing, we need to find the answers to two questions:

■ What exactly does this child find difficult?

■ How does the child need to adjust his or her thinking in order to work more effectively?

The first question needs to begin with direct observation of the child, first in class, and then individually. The assessment techniques used currently in nursery and reception classes provide an ideal basis for this – some children engage in all activities, readily answer questions, and notice for themselves details in books, including patterns in letters. They understand that print carries meaning, and explore how it does. As they move into formal phonics teaching, they understand what practitioners are telling them, and begin to use the information conveyed by letters to blend sounds, decode words, and read simple books and other short materials, such as rhymes or ditties. Teachers and assistants need to monitor progress in these early stages, and to identify which children are making progress.

This should be the starting point for systematic additional support and observation by the teacher and teaching assistants. The presence of assistants, and sometimes students or other volunteers, is crucial to collecting the evidence, as they are able to spend more time with individual children than the teacher can, noting in detail what they do and do not understand. The more detailed these notes are the better, and a similar individual approach should be taken with reading and spelling differences that appear at a later stage, for example when vocabulary begins to be more complex, or when children move to books that have more words per page and smaller print. Personal assessment notes should take into consideration a number of questions:

- What words is the child reading effortlessly?

- What words can't he or she read?

- Does the child hesitate and stumble, or read too quickly?

- Does he or she tend to guess from the first letter?

- Does the child try to sound words out letter by letter and then misread them?

- Does the child enjoy books and reading?

- Can the child express an opinion, retell a story, or anticipate events in it, with support if necessary?

- Are there any obvious limitations in the child's speaking and listening?

- Are there any signs of visual stress?

- Does the child have behavioural difficulties?

The first five questions are key technical points, and important for the following reasons.

■ What words is the child reading effortlessly?

This tells us which words, if any, the child has learned and stored in long-term memory. It is rare that a child cannot recognise a single word, even if it is just cat. This gives something to praise and build on.

■ What words can't he or she read?

We need very specific evidence, gained from direct individual observation. The aim of teaching will be to help the child adjust his or her thinking, and this can only be done if we know exactly what is going wrong. Knowing which words are causing trouble, and precisely what error is being made with them, tells us the adjustment in thinking we need to aim for.

■ Does the child hesitate and stumble, or read too quickly?

Both show that the child is not using the information provided by letters effectively. Reading too quickly often results in compounding an error, as the reader tries to force subsequent text to make sense of the misread word, rather like a weak jigsaw player might bang a piece with his fist to try to make it fit. Hesitation and stumbling show a lack of confidence and skill in using the information from the letters, and are generally a sign of unhappiness in reading.

■ Does he or she tend to guess from the first letter?

When we read, we need to use everything the letters tell us, though we don't believe the letters tell us everything. This type of error is quite common for children who have had little phonic teaching, or patchy teaching that focuses on the first letter only.

■ Does the child try to sound words out letter by letter and then misread them?

This error results from poorly focused phonics teaching that gives the idea that sounding words out one letter at a time is all we need to do. In reality, letters often work in groups, and one letter sometimes gives us information about another letter, so this over-simplification cannot work. Criticism of phonics based on the fact that words can't always be sounded out one letter at a time is quite valid – if children are being taught that this is what they should do.

CASE STUDY

Paul's difficulty with sounding the letters

Paul was seven, and had been educated in British schools abroad. He had been assessed as dyslexic by a leading practitioner, and had had two years of individual private teaching based on phonics. Paul tried to read from the *Neale Analysis of Reading Ability* (1997) by sounding each letter, attaching a particle of voice sound to each, and then guessing what word seemed most like the sounds he had produced. When he came to the letter *k*, he called out *kicking ke*, misusing a description sometimes used to differentiate *k* and *c*. *T-h-e* he read as 'ten'. Sounding words out in this way led to errors in very nearly every word, and my first task was to stop him doing it.

The one word Paul could read after sounding it out was cat. So, I got *The Cat in the Hat* (Dr Seuss, 2007/1957), pointed to cat and asked him to read it. As soon as he started sounding it, I stopped him, and said that from now on we were not going to call out the sound of each letter as we read, as that was preventing him from reading.

Me: What was the word?

Paul: Cat.

Me: Good.

Next, I took some plastic letters, and asked Paul to make cat, which he did.

Me: What was the word again?

Paul: Cat.

So far, so good. I substituted h for the c.

Me: What is the word?

Paul drew breath as if to sound the word out, caught my eye and said 'hat'.

Me: Good.

Now we switched the *c* and *h* around, with Paul saying the word correctly each time, and I went back to the book and pointed to *sat*.

Me: What is the word?

Paul: Sat.

Me: Very good.

Paul did not try to sound words one letter at a time again. He had successfully adjusted his thinking, and taken the first step towards Dame Marie Clay's 'construction of inner control' (1991). In the second phase of the lesson, we repeated the process with the first page of the book, which he read successfully.

The two middle questions – 'Does the child enjoy books and reading?' and 'Can the child express an opinion, retell a story, or anticipate events in it, with support if necessary?' – reflect the fact that learning to read is a social as well as an intellectual undertaking. Children do not start with an equal chance here, and some meet books and expressive language in school for the first time. This social dimension needs to be borne in mind throughout additional reading teaching. If children cannot read words they cannot read anything, but the words are a gateway to intellectual and personal achievement. The Conservative minister John Patton, who said that reading was 'not a voyage of self-discovery', was never more wrong.

If there are any concerns with the last three areas ('Are there any obvious limitations in the child's speaking and listening?', 'Are there any signs of visual stress?' and 'Does the child have behavioural difficulties?'), we need to share our observations with parents and find out how far they correspond with their own experience. Questions to parents should include:

■ Has the child ever suffered from glue ear or any other hearing difficulty?

This is important, as any interference to the perception of sounds may have influenced the child's language even if the condition has been treated. The main danger is developing a habit of taking shortcuts as a result of not hearing the complete sound of each word. The child may then project these shortcuts onto the words they read, and this often leads to an assessment that they are dyslexic. A very high proportion of children who are subsequently described as dyslexic have experienced some form of interruption to language development before the age of five, which parents often do not mention as they believe it has been dealt with.

CASE STUDY

Timothy's hearing problem

Timothy was ten, and his parents were worried about his prospects on transfer to secondary school. Timothy's spoken language and understanding were good, but he had real problems with reading and spelling. Timothy made very good progress in the early stages of learning with me, which was based on phonics, but ran into difficulty with longer words. He would consistently leave out parts of the middle of the word – for example, saying 'castrophe' for *catastrophe*, 'compition' for *competition*. Timothy's mother said that he had had a serious hearing problem at around the age of two, which showed itself through his behaviour – he would not do as he was asked, and threw tantrums. Doctors found that he couldn't clearly hear what his parents were saying to him, and his behaviour and hearing improved after they fitted grommets. Because of the long interval between the treatment of the hearing difficulty and beginning teaching, it is not possible to relate specific problems to specific aspects of the hearing difficulty. It is, however, clear that the interruption to Timothy's hearing made the clear identification of sounds and their relationship to letters harder for him to learn.

■ Does the child suffer from headaches, find it difficult to settle to watch television, or have any negative reaction to fluorescent light, including the lights in large stores? Does the child lose his or her place a lot, or do words appear to move about?

Learning to read places demands on children's eyesight that will not have been made before – as we track print, we have to focus closely on a small area of our field of vision, and at the same time move our eyes systematically along lines and back to the starting point without losing our place. For some children, the process is made more difficult by sensitivity to light, particularly to fluorescent light, which operates by means of a spark flashing inside a tube at a rate of a hundred flashes per second. Most of us do not notice this flashing, but for a minority of children and adults it produces an effect which ranges from mild discomfort, which might make us less likely to enjoy reading, to very severe headaches. In the most extreme cases, Professor Arnold Wilkins (1995) has established a link between visual stress and epileptic fits.

If visual stress is contributing to reading difficulty, it will hamper the effects of whatever teaching a child is offered. Teachers therefore need to know about it, and to be ready to deal with it if it arises. The problem will not necessarily show itself in a normal eye examination, as these do not require children to use their eyes in the way we do as we read. Sometimes, too, the effect of visual stress only appears after children have been reading for some minutes, and an eye test does not involve this. The British Institute of Optometry has designed a screening kit that allows you to make an initial assessment of whether a tint might help a child (www.ioo.com). Other schemes, including The Irlen Institute (www.irlen.com) and Tintavision (www.tintavision.com), also have clear evidence of benefits to children and adults. Some teachers, who have often spent their working lives under fluorescent light, have found relief from headaches and migraine by using tinted overlays and tinted backgrounds to computer screens.

CASE STUDY

Martin, Susan and Raymond

Martin was a very well-behaved and charming boy until he went to school and started to learn to read. His behaviour then deteriorated, to the extent that he became violently destructive and tried to burn down his house. Martin was removed to an expensive private school where, some years later, a teacher tried putting a tinted overlay over a page. Martin was immediately able to learn to read, and his good behaviour and pleasant personality were restored. I met him when he was twelve. He could then read without an overlay, though more hesitantly and with about a 10 per cent loss in speed.

Susan was a teacher in an Essex primary school who found she was getting headaches while reading stories to her class. Susan's classroom was lit with fluorescent light. At a staff training course on reading, I asked if anyone had ever found reading uncomfortable, or had ever felt uncomfortable under fluorescent light. Susan said she had, and after trying a range of overlays settled on a blue one. She had no further headaches.

Raymond, a senior county inspector, was having headaches while reading documents. He found immediate and lasting benefits from a light blue overlay. He was delighted, and pronounced 'That's my colour!'

■ Does the child have behavioural difficulties?

Martin's case shows that the frustration at not being able to read can have consequences for behaviour. It is important to consider the contexts in which children do not behave as they ought, and to seek parents' views on possible causes. Any marked change in behaviour as a child starts school, particularly if he or she is not making good progress in reading, should include reading as an issue to be investigated. Success in reading and spelling should be strongly rewarded as part of any programme to improve behaviour.

Try this: adjust your computer screen

On your wordprocessor, select background colours and see if they make it more comfortable to view the screen. (For Microsoft Word, go to format, then background). If you find that one colour seems to help, vary the shade until you find the one that suits you best, then save it with your normal template – follow the instructions in Help to do this. It may also help to lower the screen brightness and contrast settings.

Adapting teaching

The first session of any additional teaching and support is crucial, and is best taught by a very experienced teacher. If a teaching assistant or less experienced teacher is to provide the main support, it will help if they sit in on this first session, and parents or carers should be invited too. This will help to ensure that subsequent teaching and help at home use the same techniques and principles. The lesson should be individual, and the child must feel that he or she is supported personally and professionally, and is going to do well. To do this, some significant impact on thinking needs to be made in the first lesson, and the child must feel that they have learned something. Almost always, the main weakness will be in not using the information from the letters effectively, whether by guessing from the first letter or taking shortcuts. Explaining this, and discussing with the child what approaches might help him or her to use the letters more effectively, is a key part of almost every initial lesson I teach.

Why individual teaching?

Where possible, the initial lesson should be individual. We are helping a child to adjust his or her thinking, and each child needs to do this in his or her own way. Not all have the same strengths, make the same mistakes, or have the same path to understanding – some may have weaknesses in memory that require a lot of reinforcement with games and activities that would waste other children's time. Individual teaching is expensive, and needs therefore to work efficiently.

Adapting teaching to help weak readers and spellers does not mean setting up an alternative curriculum, or starting from scratch and grinding the child through every aspect of English spelling. There are many published teaching systems that do just that, working on the principle that, if you go over something often enough, it is bound to stick. Sometimes, these schemes give an illusion of success by having a child master a particular spelling pattern at the time that it is taught, simply because they have been focusing on it to the exclusion of all else. That approach relies on a very predictable, artificial context and does not prepare the child to identify the word in the normal course of reading. Teaching needs instead to establish patterns as part of children's thinking, so that they know when to apply them in spelling, and can interpret the information provided by letters as they read. This requires patient explanation, discussion and practice, and not adherence to the next stage in a pre-set programme, whether it is most needed or not.

The assessment system set out above gives a picture of what the child does and does not know, and the teacher may well build initial teaching and explanation into it. The starting point for teaching is then the material the child needs to read, whether in class or for pleasure. Sometimes this will be books from a reading scheme, but for older children it may well be the texts they read in class. This has the advantage of giving them two bites at the cherry, as they meet in their lessons material they have already prepared at home.

Try this: keeping information on file

Whenever a teacher uses a text in class, or prepares a worksheet, a copy is filed for the SENCO or learning support assistant. This is then used as a basis for reading lessons, preferably before the material is used in class, so that the child has an increased chance of success during the lesson.

Teaching is then based on finding something the child does know that is related to each point of difficulty, and building on it. If the spur for teaching is a particular error or pattern in errors, the basic technique is to go back from the error to a related word that the child does know, and then build up from that point. It is very rare for a child not to be able to read any words at all, but there may be a few words that are close enough to the word causing the problem to be helpful. In that case, the technique is to find another word that is *like* the unknown word, teach that in detail, and then add other examples to build up a model that the child can use to read the word. This is illustrated in the case study below.

CASE STUDY

Emily, aged six

Emily had serious difficulty with reading simple words, and could not read *sun*. I took three plastic letters, and made *run* on the table top. I then explained to Emily how each of the letters gave us a sound, and modelled blending them together slowly to make the word, encouraging Emily to join in, which she did. I then mixed the letters, and Emily put them back in the right order, reading the word again. I added *f*, and we continued the modelling with *fun*. We then switched *f* and *r*, with Emily reading the word each time, and then added *g*, then *b*. Emily was happy to play along until she'd learned it well enough to give me a little look when I went to repeat the exercise, at which point I introduced the *s*, and she read *sun* with no effort. We then returned to the book and began reading again from the beginning of the sentence.

Key points in this technique are:

- Moving away from the word that has caused the problem reduces stress and anxiety – the child isn't battling away at the problem, but looking at something new.

- The new word gives the child a pattern, and so enables him or her to learn by analogy. Successful readers often do this without prompting, but weaker readers need it to be built into the system.

- Children learn to use all of the letters in a word, and not just the first letter.

■ Working with the group of words helps reinforce the memory – each word in the pattern reinforces the others.

■ Returning to the text after working on the word makes the child re-read the word he or she has just learned, in its original context.

Overall, the effect is much like a music lesson. A child starting a new piece of music may try to read it at sight, but is not always expected to play it perfectly. Phrasing, louder or softer notes, fluency, all come with practice, and the satisfaction of playing a piece well is the result of work. It is the same with reading. It is important to choose a book that is not too easy or too hard, and that the child finds interesting. Even if they have to work hard at it, the eventual satisfaction of reading without errors is rewarding and essential.

CASE STUDY

Lillian, aged eight

Lillian is bright, and found it embarrassing that she could not read as quickly and fluently as her classmates in Germany. She did, however, know and use the basic connections between sounds and letters, and so did not need to begin from scratch. I explained to her the ways in which letters worked, both individually and in groups, and how some letters gave us information about the sounds of other letters. I also gave an outline explanation of why letters didn't always behave as we expected. We then began with books from the Woodpeckers strand of the Oxford Reading Tree, which are phonically based, and used the techniques above until she could read each book fluently and confidently. From time to time, I would engage Lillian in conversation about some other matter, such as her birthday or pets, and once her mind was thoroughly off the subject of reading, I would jump back to a word she'd found difficult and ask her to read it. Lillian got used to this trick, and was soon outwitting me by learning the words and getting them right.

It took us two sessions to read all of the Woodpeckers. When my wife and I visited Lillian and her parents in Munich a few weeks later, Lillian was tackling new material confidently, and a few weeks later we received a postcard with the message '... she read out loud in class last week with no mistakes ... Her visit to you has had more than reading benefits, it has unlocked her little world and she has joined the rest of us.' Lillian is now in her teens and reads the Brontës and Jane Austen.

Memory

Children studied in Professor Katharine Perera's doctoral thesis (1989) only began to phrase their reading naturally, rather than bark at print, once they were reading sixty to seventy words a minute accurately. It is not possible to work out words from scratch at such a rate, and so reading at this speed, which is still under half that of a typically fluent adult reader, depends on having words stored in the memory, ready to be recalled at sight rather than worked out. Almost all people with literacy difficulties have weaknesses in their use of their memory, but it is possible to help them to improve this. Memory work can be built into teaching at each stage by teaching children the importance of memory, and having them make conscious efforts to organise their own memory and to remember words in groups with similar letter patterns. I build the techniques detailed below into all of my individual teaching.

Try this: improving memory

Each student has a notebook, which includes their reading record. As they read to me, I use the technique described in Emily's example above, and keep a note of the words we've worked on, so that each page has a series of little lists of words with recurring patterns. Towards the end of the lesson, I refer back to the words we've learned to check if the learner remembers them without hesitation. We might work on this so that if a child can't read one word on a list, another may act as a prompt. If the child can read all of the words without hesitation at the end of the session, we do no more for the moment, though I will probably go back to the lists at the start of the next lesson, just to check.

If there is still hesitation, or if the child is still making mistakes, I print off a grid (see the accompanying CD for a selection) and insert words into it. I place them at random, except that I avoid putting two words with the same pattern next to each other. We then play a simple game, with me calling out grid co-ordinates and the child reading the words in the grid. If they get one wrong, I move to a word with the same pattern that they are likely to get right. Once they have got it, I call out the co-ordinates of other words with the same pattern for reinforcement. Any stubborn words can be inserted into a later grid, and reinforced by further explanation. Sue Palmer, author of *Toxic Childhood* (2006), found this technique very helpful in work with her daughter (see 'As easy as ABC really', www.tes.co.uk, archive, 1.3.1996).

Once the approach is established, I vary it by having a conversation with the learner, towards the middle of the lesson, on some topic that has nothing to do with what we've been reading about. It could be football, what they'd like for their birthday, anything. Once I'm sure that their mind is off the subject of the lesson, I switch back without warning to the words we've been learning and ask the child to read them. I find that they soon get used to this, and rehearse the words in their minds so that I won't have the satisfaction of catching them out. I've learned to accept the disappointment with good grace.

Stages in learning and remembering words

A child who has worked on a word and then forgets it has rarely forgotten it so completely that it is as if he or she has never known it. Peter, in Chapter 2, was able to pick out a named word from other words before he could read it for himself, and he could not have done this if he had not retained some trace of it in his memory. This partial memory, I have found, tends to follow these stages:

1. Child or adult needs substantial help in constructing a word from its letters.

2. They read the word after a prompt, or help with part rather than all of it.

3. A word is misread, but the learner corrects it immediately or after reading it in context.

4. The learner reads the word after hesitation, without error or assistance.

5. The word is read without hesitation.

Not every learner uses all stages, and once past the initial stages, stops along the way become less frequent, so that readers well on the way to fluency can often go from needing a prompt or partial help to reading a word without hesitation once they've grasped the pattern or point of difficulty. Each time a word is read without hesitation, the store of words in the learner's long-term memory is increased. As a result, the amount of work that has to go into decoding is reduced, and the resources available to the reader are increased, so that fluency can grow.

Sustaining interest

You can keep learners' interest, and avoid additional literacy support developing into a separate curriculum, by basing the work on the reading and writing a child does in class, and on an adult learner's own interests. There are two main advantages:

■ As basic patterns, both regular and irregular, run throughout the language, you will meet them in this material without having to go to specially constructed schemes. This allows you to concentrate on each learner's specific areas of weakness without wasting time going over what he or she already knows.

■ The child will then meet the material again in class, which provides more practice. The adult will meet the material in the course of their reading and writing for leisure or work. If possible, try to put in the extra teaching just before children meet the material in class. This gives them a better chance of succeeding in class first time, and is better for morale than helping them after they have struggled. Basing spelling lessons on the learner's writing avoids the problem of them learning words for a test, in which they are tested out of context, and then forgetting them. The normal run of the learner's writing shows you what they need to work on in practice, as well as providing a running record of achievement.

Identifying progress

The starting point is the result of the initial assessments you have carried out, and any additional notes. These may include some age-standardised features. The end point should be when you and the learner are satisfied that they are reading and spelling as well as they should be. This result is subjective, but that does not mean that it is a matter of unsupported individual opinion. Your records will show what they were struggling with, and are now getting right. Teachers and parents may note increased confidence, perhaps accompanied by merit awards. Notes such as that from Lillian's mother (above) are important,

Grids for word practice

Some words have been added to the first as an example – there is no need to use every square. Expand grids to meet the needs of the learner.

	A	B	C	D	E
1	hat	met	pat		tap
2		cat		pet	
3	sat		can		get

Name: Date

	A	B	C	D	E
1					
2					
3					

Name: **Date**

	A	B	C	D	E
1					
2					
3					
4					
5					

Name: **Date**

	1	2	3	4	5	6
A						
B						
C						
D						
E						
F						

as they give a dimension of evidence that tests would not detect. There may, and should, be success in national and standardised test scores, though these have to be interpreted in the light of individual needs. It is not enough to have someone reading at the level expected for their age in a test if their abilities indicate that they should be achieving more than this. In some cases, the benefits are very long-term – one student, who learned to read at ten, is now studying philosophy and languages at university. Another, who had reached his twenties unable to read, can now read the print he meets at work and handle correspondence from his bank and health club.

The following signs of progress need to be seen in terms of each student's needs and abilities:

- Correcting own errors without prompting – a key indicator of growing control.

- A reduced error rate in reading, with good learning of new features and words.

- Faster, more fluent reading of texts in class or at work.

- A lower rate of spelling error in normal writing.

- Reading voluntarily, for pleasure or instruction.

- Noticing and reading environmental print more easily.

- Fewer headaches, better sleep or behaviour.

- Improved results in school, national or standardised tests.

Test scores are placed last not because they are unimportant but because they follow from the other indicators.

Teaching assistants

The success of Ruth Miskin's work (www.ruthmiskinliteracy.com/testimonials .aspx) at Kobi Nazrul school shows that well-trained teaching assistants can work to the same standard as qualified teachers; the main difference between assistants and teachers lies in the scope of their work. By studying the examples above, and working with experienced teachers, assistants will learn which are the most important, and how to explain them to the children. If the work is carefully recorded and collated, it can be built into GNVQ assessment, as set out in Chapter 8. Assistants also need access to all of the records and external assessments of the children they support. The SENCO should discuss these and make sure that they understand them and the use of confidential information.

Parents

Close involvement of parents from the start gives three advantages:

- They know what you are doing about their child's difficulties.

- They can provide information that the school would not otherwise have.

- They can use the same techniques as the school.

Where possible, it helps to have a parent sit in on a lesson. This has to be handled tactfully, but it is important for the parent to see exactly what the child is doing, so that they can support the work. Seating the parent alongside the child, out of the child's line of sight, but where the parent can see the text, helps avoid embarrassment. A parent was present during all of the examples given above. I sometimes have to have a word in advance so that the parent knows not to join in too much, but they are always welcome to join in praise.

Once a parent has seen the approach, a home–school reading record keeps everyone in touch. It is important to cover all dimensions of reading in the record – children should enjoy the books that go home, and the parent should note their response. They should also note any words that are read fluently, particularly new words, and any that the child stumbles over. The child's comments should be included too, with help if needed. Some children like to add a smiley face. If the teacher, assistant and parent use the same notebook, everyone is up to date with what everyone else is doing and, most of all, what progress is or is not being made. Over time, this notebook builds up a personal record of achievement for each child, and becomes a valuable source of encouragement, showing the child how far they have come. This can be particularly helpful to boys.

Building support into your normal school provision

As we know in advance that some children will have difficulty with literacy, it makes sense to plan provision in advance, and to organise resources so that they can be applied as early as possible. Every teacher, assistant and volunteer needs to know the school's approach to reading, and to understand its organisation. Each child who is noted as having any difficulty with aspects of reading as they are taught is then placed on a class register, and extra help allocated until the problem is solved. This may be a very short process – if teaching is carefully focused on dealing with a specific problem, and on helping children adjust their thinking, it can work very quickly.

Extra reading teaching can be organised at any time during the school day, and may be either individual or group work depending on need. This takes a long-term view of children's entitlement to a broad and balanced curriculum – over the eleven years of their school career to GCSE, they can only have access to such a curriculum if they can read well enough to handle the material. For some children, group work may be better than whole-class teaching from the beginning. The National Literacy Strategy's literacy hour was based on all children in the class taking part in the lesson, whether or not they could understand it – this caused particular problems in the later years of primary school, where teachers were encouraged to pitch work at a demanding level for the highest-attaining children in the class. Grouping children according to their learning needs from the beginning enables teachers to match work to their needs, and saves children the frustration of being presented with work they do not understand.

FURTHER READING

Remedial Techniques in Basic School Subjects, Grace Fernald (1943) New York: McGraw-Hill. Written before the age of computers, Fernald's insights into adapting teaching methods to tackle learning differences still repay study, in mathematics as well as literacy. The original edition is recommended, as it includes remarkable case studies.

Errors and Expectations: A Guide for the Teacher of Basic Writing, Mina Shaugnessy(ed.) (1977) New York: Oxford University Press. A practical, highly informative description of work in the basic writing department at City College, New York. Particularly valuable on the discrepancies between students' capabilities and talents, and their ability to express themselves in formal English.

Dyslexia, Speech and Language, 2nd edn. Margaret Snowling and Joy Stackhouse (eds) (2005) Chichester: Wiley. A very useful update on research evidence, particularly on memory, which suggests further lines of enquiry and will be invaluable to students.

CHAPTER 9

Professional Development

> **This chapter will:**
>
> ■ Consider the principles of successful training
> ■ Help you assess the training your school needs
> ■ Provide a framework for an audit and preparation
> ■ Show how to plan a successful course
> ■ Consider the needs of teaching assistants
> ■ Show how to build CPD into evaluation and planning for the whole school

What makes a good course?

Successful courses depend on having something useful to say, and saying it as we like to be spoken to ourselves – clearly, cordially, and in proper English rather than jargon. As course leaders, we should not expect teachers to agree with every word we say. We must be prepared to take questions as they arise, ensure that we have sufficient knowledge to answer fully wherever possible, and admit it when we can't. There is no shame in not knowing everything, and we can always offer to check and get back to a colleague later.

Most good courses have the following characteristics:

■ The leader knows the subject in real depth.

■ Colleagues' views are taken into account, in advance if possible.

■ The content is practical, and meets the needs of teachers and their pupils.

- Sessions are pacey, not too long, and finish on time.

- An atmosphere of co-operation and respect is established and maintained.

- A foundation is laid for further development.

The first point requires a great deal of preparation and experience from course leaders. If it is not met, they will be reduced to telling people what they already know. . They must not bluff or fudge. In literacy work, they need to know the background to the phonics debate, including the arguments that have been put forward against phonics, and the nature of regular and irregular patterns in English. If they don't, they may meet a question that points out a contradiction between the language, or patterns of learning observed in a class, and something they have just said. If that happens, the only path is to acknowledge the error, but it is much better to avoid it in the first place. To do this, the leader must be well-read.

The second and third points are linked. The audit (see below) tells you what your colleagues do and do not know, and it should be clear from this what your main focus needs to be. The task then is to think clearly and to present your points succinctly and in the right order. I use a simple Powerpoint presentation for this, with bullet points on a notebook framework, without gimmicks like having points flash onto the screen one at a time, or float into place as if from heaven. I then talk round the bullet points. The approach borrows from Churchill (see Cooke 1973), who used to work hard to edit his speeches down to a series of main points, in effect bullet points, which would be typed out on cards. Compressing what you want to say in this way focuses your mind on what is and is not essential, and then frees you to add points as they come up, either in discussion during the course or in informal conversations with staff. Churchill's maxim that short words are better than long ones is also important. It is easy to drift into a register of language that is too far removed from normal English, and the more this happens, the less effective the talk. To put complex matters into simple English, we need to understand them in depth – jargon does not signify expertise.

When I began advisory work in Essex in the 1980s, practical work on literacy courses was derided as 'tips for teachers'. In fact, the more practical advice and guidance on technique that can be built into a course, the better. A course leader can expect the audience to have constantly in their minds the questions *How can I do this?*, *Is this going to work for my class?*, *Have I got time for it?* and possibly, *Can*

I afford it? As phonics knowledge alone is not enough to enable children to read many English words, the first two questions are certain to arise in phonics courses. I have found the following points helpful in answering them:

- The brain adapts to combine phonic work with other types of information from letters. As we learn to read, we do not just apply phonics, but interpret what letters tell us.

- We use what the letters tell us, but we don't believe the letters tell us everything. Some things we have to know for ourselves.

- The language is a thousand years old, and if we were that old we'd have a few wrinkles. This is a particularly useful maxim in explaining irregularity; as we have seen in Chapter 1, the biggest single source of irregularity is the historical event of the Norman conquest, while most of the rest is rooted in changes in pronunciation over centuries, which are not reflected in spelling.

- To help a child remember, I do not teach a child a word he or she has just got wrong, but another that is like it. I then introduce other, similar words and, once the pattern is established, return to the word that has caused the problem. Children almost always then get it right. This is a most useful 'tip for teachers', and almost always generates nods and smiles.

Preparation, reading and organisation are the keys to a pacey presentation. This is particularly important if people are coming to your course after a hard day's work. Remember that with a group of thirty colleagues, you are using an hour of human life every two minutes. Work out your timing carefully. Leaving the last five minutes for questions gives you a buffer, and your colleagues will thank you inwardly for finishing two minutes early rather than two minutes late. You may think you'll be forgiven for running over time; if your colleagues really like you, you may be, but don't count on it.

What training do teachers of phonics need?

A course that enables teaching staff to understand and use new material well is successful, whether it lasts an hour or two days. A course that is longer than it needs to be is a waste of time, though this does not mean we should rush. We must leave time for questioning and professional discussion. A course that is too short, or that does not provide sufficient support to teachers and teaching assistants who have limited or ineffective previous use of phonics, will also leave gaps in understanding; this *always* results in limited teaching ability. The late Professor Ted Wragg (Wragg and Brown 2001) noted that primary children valued explanation above all other characteristics of good teaching, and we cannot explain things if we do not understand them ourselves. For these reasons, the co-ordinator and headteacher – who will have additional, perhaps confidential, information on the strengths and weaknesses of teaching – should consider exactly what the school needs, and follow up initial training with monitoring and further support where it is needed.

There is no inherent reason why a school should not organise its own training, but it may help to use an outside trainer for these reasons:

- The co-ordinator or headteacher may not have time to prepare a complete course.

- An outside trainer should be more experienced, and should present well.

- Using an outside trainer gives the headteacher and co-ordinator flexibility to gauge the staff's response and to plan further work.

- If some staff are not convinced of the need for phonics, an outside trainer can act as a lightning conductor – ideas can be discussed and challenged without staff feeling they are criticising their colleagues.

Check out external trainers personally, by consulting trusted colleagues, by meeting them or by attending all or part of a course. Trainers will invariably be pleased to help, and should be able to provide references. You must ensure that the trainer is fully briefed about your school's needs, and about any aspects that need particularly careful handling. This does not always require a visit, but should be more than a paper exercise: take the time for a substantial phone conversation with your trainer, and do not hesitate to book and pay for a site visit if you need it. The greatest cost in any course is your time staff's time, and your own.

The co-ordinator

Rose (2006: 50) recommends that each school should have a senior member of staff with detailed knowledge and understanding of phonics to act as co-ordinator; headteachers who are specialists in the field may take on this role themselves. Whoever acts as co-ordinator needs to be fully involved in preparation, planning, training and monitoring. They need to know the material in detail, and as a minimum this should include:

- The school's scheme of work and resources.

- The National Curriculum and Early Years Curriculum.

- *The Rose Report* (Rose 2006) and DfES guidance.

- The range of phonics materials available.

- The Handbook for the core scheme.

- The Handbook to *Read, Write Inc.* if another core scheme is chosen.

Read, Write Inc. benefits from Ruth Miskin's experience as a highly effective headteacher as well as a reading specialist. It should be read carefully for its guidance on organising the class, particularly for questioning, support for weaker pupils, and time management. The author's recommendation that the co-ordinator should have three hours per week to monitor and manage the introduction of phonics should be seen as an extension of training, and not as a way of checking up on colleagues. Managers need to know what is and is not working for *their* children, and monitoring is the only way to find this out.

Preparation and audit

An audit is essential, but should not be time-consuming. It should include:

- Schemes of work

- Resources

- Data from tests and other assessments, including samples of work and reading

- Evidence from lesson observations

- The views of teachers and teaching assistants

- The views of governors.

The first four items can be covered quickly by the co-ordinator and head-teacher. The following two questions need to be applied to resources and schemes of work:

- How well is this aspect/resource working?

- If it is less than excellent, what could we do to improve it?

Lesson observation evidence may be confidential to the headteacher. It shows two important factors: the effectiveness or ineffectiveness of teaching, and the extent to which phonics are used. It is not uncommon for there to be little or no phonics teaching beyond the infant school, and it is important to establish this in order to demonstrate to teaching staff what phonics can contribute to their work. Samples of work can usefully include hearing a sample of children read and discussing with them what they find easy and difficult, how they approach a word they don't know, and what help they are receiving. Ofsted's normal sampling technique for work and readers was to take two average, two above average, and two below average pupils from each class. Provided the children are chosen accurately, this yields a workable sample from a class in reading and writing from roughly an hour's work. The headteacher and co-ordinator together should be able to complete a key stage in half a day at most.

To gather teachers' views, I recommend photocopying the Audit of Staff Opinion form (on the accompanying CD) and distributing it at a staff meeting, with 10 minutes for colleagues to fill it in. This ensures a virtually complete response with no chasing-up. All teachers' views should be included, whether or not they currently use phonics. If anyone asks for more time, ask them to do as much as they can now and to send in more later. The goal at this stage is to collect key points rather than fine detail. Teaching assistants whose work involves reading may also bring useful experience to the audit; for those who do not work with reading, I recommend that their views be gathered by the co-ordinator.

Audit of staff opinion: Phonics

Name: Class:

What phonic work do you use:

a) for reading?

b) for spelling?

How important do you see phonic work in these areas, and why?

What are the main strengths in your current use of phonics?

Are there any areas that need development? If so, which?

Are there any important aspects of reading and spelling that need attention, and that phonics does not tackle?

What would be your priorities for developing phonic work?

(Please continue on the back of this form if necessary.)

Planning and running the course

The audit gives an outline of what a school is doing, what the staff think, and how effective the work is. All of these factors, and particularly the last, influence the design of training. A school that is already making good use of phonics, and has evidence of high achievement, does not need to run a course introducing phonics from scratch or to send staff on external briefings. An audit is still worthwhile in such schools, but as part of the normal cycle of evaluation.

If training is needed, timing is likely to range from a half day to a maximum of two days. A half-day course, which may also take the form of two staff meetings, allows time to present the results of the audit and the conclusions drawn by senior management. A half day also allows time for teaching staff to raise questions, examine new resources and for summing up at the end. For most schools that will be sufficient, unless there is a need for wholesale revision of current schemes of work; in that case, teachers will probably appreciate time to begin this with their class during the afternoon, followed by a brief concluding session. The extension of the course to a whole day is an important decision. The afternoon needs a genuine and slightly different focus to sustain interest. To provide this, the co-ordinator and headteacher must consider in detail the work needed in each key stage, or other group. This needs to be agreed with a group leader, with clear targets for what is to be achieved by the end of the afternoon, and a focused review.

The one successful two-day course I know is Ruth Miskin's introduction to *Read, Write Inc.* I have attended both days of this course and can recommend it for schools adopting her system. The first day is spent introducing basic principles of phonics work, and running through key issues of planning, teaching and organisation, while the second involves greater detail and more advanced features, including the innovative features in her series of storybooks. With this exception, my experience is that most courses are too long – particularly when they tell experienced teachers things they already know – and that training can be completed in one day at most.

Outline programme for a half-day or 1-day course

9.30   School audit: findings and next steps

9.50   *The Rose Report* and new guidance on phonics

10.00   Proposed changes to resources, schemes of work and planning proce-dures, management and monitoring arrangements

10.30   Coffee

11.00   Hands-on work by key stage, or by the school's own staff groupings, on resources, schemes of work and other planning needed to put changes into practice

12.00   Concluding session: what is clearly in place, and what remains to be done?

12.30   Lunch

Extension for full day course:

As half-day until 11.00 a.m., then

11.00   Hands-on work by key stage as above, with additional time for evalu-ating resources

12.30   Lunch

1.30   Rewriting schemes of work and planning, by year group

3.00   Concluding session

Teaching assistants

Since the early 1990s, the role of teaching assistants has been developed and extended so that they are now a key part of every school's provision. The range of learning and behavioural needs faced by schools is such that they could not function without assistants, and the assistant is often the main source of in-depth individual help and encouragement for children who need support.

Teaching assistants tend to work with individual children or small groups, while the teacher is responsible for planning and organising the learning of a whole class. Wherever possible, we should aim to have assistants work to the same standard as teachers. To achieve this, assistants must be fully involved in school performance management and professional development, and the training they receive must be closely related to the school's literacy provision and to the children they actually teach. Sending assistants outside school for training is expensive and inherently less effective. Not only is the course likely to be some way removed from a school's own systems, but assistants' work is so crucial to the smooth running of classes that most can't be spared. It should also not be taken for granted that they can give up their personal time without difficulty. Each school needs, therefore, to ensure that its assistants understand its systems for teaching reading, and how they meet the demands of its own children. This training can be certified under the NVQ framework for assistants and higher-level assistants. Not all of it need be formal – including assistants in discussions, encouraging them to ask questions, and taking time to explain issues in the context of the needs of the children they are working with are equally helpful.

Teaching assistants spend most time with children for whom learning is not straightforward. The skills they need are summarised in the box below.

Teaching assistants need to know and understand:

- the phonic principles of English spelling

- the major irregular features and their causes

- the school's core reading schemes and other resources, including ICT

- patterns of learning in reading and spelling

- the learning difficulties they are working with, and the best teaching techniques to use to tackle them

- the school's assessment systems, and how their work contributes to them

- the social and emotional needs of their pupils.

In the early 1990s, I ran a pilot course for teaching assistants for the DfES. The course was based in schools, with a weekly mentoring session for assistants with the headteacher, using a Handbook which covered each of a list of skills required by the DfES. Assistants chose two children they were working with, and each week either prepared for a mentoring session by using the techniques it covered with these children or followed up the previous week's mentoring session. They kept notes of their work with each child, building up a portfolio that met the requirement to assess each of the skills they were demonstrating. This also enabled them to see the relevance of each piece of work, to evaluate it critically, and to apply it for the benefit of their pupils. As the course was accredited for Higher Education, assistants built up their understanding by reading beyond the immediate requirements of each unit. This format allowed assistants to be trained to national standards – it was externally assessed by Middlesex University and HMI – without taking them out of school apart from two twilight sessions per term, which were required by the DfES. The only advantage to these sessions was to allow assistants to meet students from other schools, and this could easily be achieved by a meeting of all assistants in a school cluster. It showed that, provided the format was clear, it was possible to train assistants to a high standard within the constraints of their conditions of employment and without encroaching on their personal time.

Here is a suggested way to develop assistants' knowledge and experience of using phonics:

- Decide on a mentor – normally either the co-ordinator or headteacher.

- Decide on timing of mentoring sessions – a half-hour per week would be the minimum.

- Each assistant selects one or two students whom they see regularly.

- The mentor devises a series of mentoring sessions covering the points in the box above.

- For each mentoring session, there is a preparation and follow-up activity. The assistant carries these out, and their work provides a focal point for each mentoring session, minimising prep time for the mentor.

- The assistant keeps notes on each activity in a folder. The mentor checks the notes, and suggests further work where needed. The key criteria are that the assistant has understood the work and applied it successfully.

- The folder contributes to the continuing assessment of each child. If it is integrated with NVQ requirements, it provides the basis of a school-based qualification for each assistant. To do this, the school needs to arrange with an NVQ provider to have the folders independently assessed, following which the mentor may also qualify as an NVQ assessor.

Make it a habit: CPD in the evaluation and planning cycle

Evaluation and planning have become associated with targets in examination and test performance, at the expense of qualitative criteria such as reading fluency and understanding. As a result, weaknesses in these areas, which are important for future achievement, may not be detected. We can avoid the problem by evaluating work in terms of direct observation of children's strengths and weaknesses as well as through test results.

The design of schemes of work in Chapter 2 includes an evaluation column in each activity, and the start of an effective evaluation and planning cycle is to make sure we all use it. This requires discipline on the part of the teacher, and systematic review by the co-ordinator and the headteacher to gather evidence of what is and is not working. Negative comments should be given equal value to positive ones. They need to be discussed, and followed up by observation. Is the weakness in the activity, or in some aspect of the way it is used? Does it affect the whole class, or some groups of pupils? The same criteria can be used to evaluate successful elements. Why is a particular feature working well? Can it – like the use of small writing boards, for example – be extended to other areas or subjects? If an approach to reading is working well in literacy in Years 5 and 6, can it be reinforced in science, or might it help children read maths questions more accurately?

The response needs to be proportionate – agreed amendments to the scheme of work might be enough, while extra training or investigation may be needed for others, particularly if it appears that a key principle has not been understood.

FURTHER READING

Teaching Assistant's Edufax, John Bald (2004) Hadleigh: Curriculum Publishing.
 Contains complete planning for a school-based course that enables teaching
 assistants and higher level teaching assistants to be trained to NVQ levels 3 and 4.

GLOSSARY

Note: Some terms are taken from academic linguistics, and it is often better to replace them with simple English words that the child can understand.

Analytic phonics – Beginning with a whole word, and identifying sounds in it. Some forms of analytic phonics limit the analysis to the initial letter.

Blending – Putting together the sounds represented by letters in order to read words.

Cluster – Two or three letters grouped together, each of which makes a distinct sound, for example *cl*am, *str*oll.

Digraph – Two letters which together make one unit of sound , for example *sh*, *ch*, *ph*, *ee*, *oo*.

Discrete – Separate and self-contained. A discrete lesson is one that focuses on one topic, sometimes in isolation.

Grapheme – A letter or group of letters representing one unit of sound, for example *sh*, *ch*, *igh*, *ough* (as in *though*). In some definitions, punctuation marks are also seen as graphemes.

Grapheme–phoneme correspondence – The relationship between sounds and the letters that represent them.

Irregularity – A departure from the most frequent correspondence between a sound and the letters representing it.

Magic *e* – A term used in some phonic schemes to describe the effect of a final *e* on the preceding vowel in words such as *made*, *here*, *cute* and so on. See *split digraph*.

Mnemonic – A device for remembering something, for example Sammy Snake for *s*, or for spelling *because*, 'big elephants can always understand small elephants'. Most mnemonics work for one word only.

Multisensory teaching – Teaching that involves action and movement, and sometimes singing, as well as looking, speaking and listening.

Onset and rime – A way of analysing single-syllable words into two parts. The first part is a consonant or consonant group, the second part is the rime, for example for *ed* in *bed*, the onset is *b*, the rime *ed*. Sometimes mistakenly described as a method of teaching reading.

Phoneme – A unit of sound, for example *cat* and *shed* have three phonemes, *c*, *a* and *t*, and *sh*, *e* and *d*.

Phonemic awareness – Awareness of individual sounds, and the ability to distinguish between them.

Phonics – Instruction that teaches the correspondences between letters and sounds, and how to use these to read and spell words.

Phonological awareness – Awareness of sounds and differences between them. This includes rhyme, and the differences between vowel (voice sounds).

Psycholinguistics – An academic discipline combining elements of linguistics and elements of psychology.

Segmenting – Breaking down a word into its sounds.

Systematic phonics – The teaching of all the major grapheme–phoneme correspondences, and they are covered in a clearly defined sequence.

Synthetic phonics – For reading: blending (synthesising) sounds to read words. Also known as 'word-building'. For spelling: writing words by representing sounds with letters or groups of letters.

Split digraph – Two letters, which represent one sound, 'split' by inserting one, or occasionally more than one, consonant, for example *oe* in *toe* is split in words such as *tore*, *tone*, *token*.

Trigraph – Three letters denoting a vowel sound, for example b*eau*tiful.

VC, CVC, CCVC – Shorthand for letter patterns: vowel–consonant (VC) as in *am*, consonant–vowel–consonant (CVC) as in *Sam*, and consonant–consonant–vowel–consonant (CCVC) as in *spam*.

Vowel – A sound made by the voice. We often call the letters *a e i o u* vowels – this can be misleading, as *y* and *w* also represent voice sounds, and some vowels need more than one letter to represent them, for example sh*ow*. The problem can be avoided by referring to the letters representing vowels as *vowel letters*.

APPENDIX: KEY PATTERNS IN ENGLISH SPELLING

These lists cover the main spelling patterns in English, with five or six words for each. This is a basic reference point, and it is helpful to add words or patterns that emerge in the course of students' work.

There are three sections:

1. Basic patterns: direct correspondence between sounds and letters, with a small numbers of words that use an extra letter.

2. Second stage patterns: interactions between letters, and regular letters groups in which letters do not represent their frequent sounds.

3. Common irregular and historical patterns.

Section 1: Basic patterns

Consonant–vowel–consonant, vowel–consonant	
a	
cat fat hat mat at	can fan man dan an
cap tap rap map gap	sad bad mad dad tad
ham Sam jam dam ram	bag rag tag nag jag
e	
bed red fed led	hen ten men Ben (with extra letter) when
pet set net let wet met	leg beg peg

i	
bin pin sin win in	bit pit fit sit it
did hid lid sid rid	him dim Jim rim Tim
dig big pig wig fig	his is
six fix mix	
o	
hot lot not rot cot pot	dog log bog fog jog hog
nod god cod rod hod	don on (with extra letter) gone John
hop	box

pop top mop lop	fox cox pox
rob job lob hob (with extra letter) knob	
u	
cup pup sup	cut hut but nut rut
run bun sun fun gun	mum hum rum tum sum
rug bug hug mug tug	bus us
Extra letter at the end of the word	
ss	*ll*
lass mass	(*ll* almost always changes pronunciation of *a*, and sometimes changes the pronuncuation of *u*)

mess	
less	ball
press	call
dress	wall
	tall
	all
miss	
hiss	bell
kiss	well
	tell
moss	fell
loss	sell
toss	
boss	kill
ross	will
	till
fuss	hill
cuss	fill
	dull
	mull
	gull
	hull
	pull
	bull
	full
ck	*ng*
back	rang
lack	bang
hack	sang
tack	hang
(with extra letter) whack	
	ring
neck	sing
heck	wing

peck (with extra letter) wreck	ding king
tick pick sick lick (with extra letter) quick	long song pong Hong Kong (with extra letter) wrong
sock lock tock rock (with extra letter) knock	sung lung hung
suck tuck luck duck buck muck	

Basic pattern consonant groups at beginning or end of word. The number of combinations here is very large, and these are only a few examples.

Two-letter groups

chop chap chin chess much such rich	thank think bath path that then this with	shed ship ship shut shell fish wish push	fashion cushion (in this position, *sh* is unusual, but can be learned here)

blip blob blast black bled	bran bring brat brag bread (*ea* group)	clip clop class clap clan	crab crust crisp (extra letter) crumb cross
drop drip drink drum drag	dwell dwarf (awkward *a* after *w*) dwindle (*dw* is scarce)	flip flop flap flan flag	frog frill fred frost
glad glum gloss glen glut	grip grab grin grub grit	plum plastic plant please (*ea* group) plenty	prim press prom prod pretty (extra letter and awkward *e*)
stop star stall still sting	scarf scum scan scar school (extra letters)	skill skip skin skunk skull	spin spill spar sport spend
the they then this that thought (*ough* group)	*h* here is not silent – you can feel it if you hold your hand in front of your mouth as you say the word wheel when where what who (*w* not pronunced)		

Three-letter groups (note that the third letter is usually *r*)			
scrap screw scrum scrimp scrub	shrimp shrub shred shrill shrug	spring sprout sprint sprig sprat	square squib squirrel squid (awkward *a*) squad squash
strap strip stroke stripe string	three (extra *e*) throw through (*ough* group) throb thrust		

Section 2: Second stage patterns

Second level patterns: soft *c* and *g*			
face	cent	circus	cycle
race	centre	circle	bicycle
place	cell	city	tracy
lace	centigrade	citizen	cypher
pace	century	(extra letter)	
		circuit	
page	gem	giraffe	energy
rage	gel	giant	Egypt
stage	gentle	ginger	gym
cage	general	gin	gymnast
age	George	gipsy	gymnasium
Note: Soft *g* is inconsistent – it doesn't operate with *get, girl, give, gift, begin*			
Second level patterns: vowel groups (or vowel digraphs)			
rain	day	jaw	august
train	may	law	autumn
nail	pay	saw	author
paint	play	lawn	haunt
(shortcut)	way	yawn	launch
again	away	awful	
sea (long *e*)	head (short *e*)	bee	feet
eat	dead	see	meet
beat	bread	tree	green
heat	instead	free	week
cheat	steady	feel	cheek
seat	ready	feed	sleep
look	goal	out	now
cook	coal	about	cow
book	oak	loud	down
took	coat	cloud	brown

nook	road	sound	clown
	toast	ground	crowd
	float	mouth	flower
oil	boy		
soil	joy		
boil	toy		
coin	enjoy		
point	royal		

Second level patterns: final *e* (or split digraphs)

bake	fine	bone	use
cake	nine	hole	amuse
game	shine	pole	cube
name	five	nose	tube
gate	drive	rose	cute
plate	life	broke	flute
tale	wipe	smoke	duke
brave	smile	home	mule
shape	white		tune

The construction is less common e-e in short words - *here, Pete*. It is used in many two-syllable words – *complete, compete, concrete, athlete, delete.*

Second level patterns: *igh*   ***al***   ***our***

high	light	almost	flavour
sigh	sight	also	harbour
thigh	might	always	colour
	bright	walnut	behaviour (extra
	fight	halt	letter)
	(extra letter)		armour
	height		humour

Second level patterns: vowel plus *r*				
girl	fern	fur	car	for
fir	kerb	burn	arm	cork
stir	termn	turn	harm	stork
bird	after	church	far	short
thirst	butter	curl	cart	sport
shirt	sister	Saturday	dart	
birthday	under	Thursday	dark	

Second level patterns: *tion*

Long *a*	Long *o*	Short vowels (extra letter before *tion*)
station	notion	action
nation	lotion	fraction
	potion	reaction
	motion	addition
		friction
		option
		suction
		reduction
		competition
		section
		direction
		mention
ssion	*sion* (slightly softer)	*ti*
mission	television (vision)	patient
permission	explosion	essential
possession	division	partial
discussion	confusion	confidential
impression	occasion	initial
professional	decision	

ci		
special		
official		
social		
artificial		
delicious		
musician		
Second level patterns: extra letter as a wall, to stop one letter affecting another		
gu	**more** *gu*, *cu*	*dge*
guess	dialogue	badge
guitar	vague	bridge
guest	rogue	edge
guide	league	sledge
plague	biscuit	edge
guy	circuit	dodge
double letters used as a wall to keep the first vowel short		
happen	bitten	battle
happy	swimming	settle
tapped	Slipped	little
slapping	shopping	bottle
Betty	cutting	cuttlefish

Section 3: Common irregular and historical patterns

ear	*ea* (awkward sound)	*eigh*	*o* as *u* sound	*wa* (from German)
earth	bear	eight	love	was
early	pear	neigh	glove	warm
learn	tear (e.g. clothes)	neighbour	come	water
pearl	break	weigh	some	want
search	steak	weight	mother	war
hears		(height)	brother	wasp
			something	what (extra letter)

ough			*augh*	
thought	although	enough	caught	
bought	though	rough	daughter	
ought	dough	tough	naughty	
fought				
	plough	trough	laugh	
thorough	bough	cough	laughter	
borough	slough		draught	

Note: Only *through* does not have a near neighbour. Use a picture to remember it.

le (French)	*que* French	*ch* as *sh* (French)	*eau* (French)
table	antique	machine	beauty
stable	unique	parachute	beautiful
cable	boutique	bochure	*ieu* (French)
able	queue	chef	
possible	cheque	champagne	in lieu (in place of)
reasonable	technique		

ph (Greek)	Hard *ch* (Greek)	Silent *w* (Old English)	Silent *b* (Teutonic/Norse)
photograph	Christmas	wrap	lamb
elephant	chemist	wrong	climb
hyphen	chorus	wrist	dumb
phonic	school	wrinkle	plumber
alphabet	stomach	write	
geography	ache		

Silent *k* (Germanic)	*uit* (French)
know	fruit
knight	suit
knot	biscuit
knob	circuit
knit	

Adams, P. (1988) *Mrs Honey's Hat*. Swindon: Child's Play International.

Armitage, D. and Armitage, R. (1994) *The Lighthouse Keeper's Lunch*. London: Scholastic Hippo.

Bald, J. (2001) 'Slimmed Down Spelling', *Times Educational Supplement*, 25 May.

Bald, J. (2003) 'Eyes bright', *Times Educational Supplement*, 19 September.

Bald, J. (2004) *Teaching Assistant's Edufax*. Hadleigh: Curriculum Publishing.

Balmuth, M. (1982) *The Roots of Phonics: A Historical Introduction*. New York: McGraw-Hill.

Bissex, G. (1980) *Gyns at Wrk: A Child Learns to Read and Write*. Cambridge, MA: Harvard University Press.

Blake, Q. (1999) *Mr Magnolia*. London: Red Fox.

Frith, U. and Blakemore, S-J. (2005) *The Learning Brain: Lessons for Education*. Oxford: Blackwell.

Bradley, L. and Bryant, P. E. (1983) 'Categorizing sounds and learning to read – a causal connection', *Nature*, 301: 419–21.

Butler, D. (1979) *Cushla and Her Books*. London: Hodder & Stoughton.

Carle, E. (2002) *The Very Hungry Caterpillar*. London: Puffin.

Chall, J. S., Jacobs, V. A. and Baldwin, L.E. (1990) *The Reading Crisis: Why Poor Children Fall Behind*. Cambridge, MA: Harvard University Press.

Clay, M. (1991) *Becoming Literate: The Construction of Inner Control*. Auckland: Heinemann.

Concise Oxford English Dictionary (2004) CD-ROM, 11th edn. Oxford: OUP.

Cooke, A. (1973) *Alistair Cooke in America*. London: BBC Publications.

Department for Education and Skills (1998) *National Literacy Strategy, Framework for Teaching*. London: DfES.

Fernald, G. M. (1943) *Remedial Techniques in Basic School Subjects*. New York: McGraw-Hill.

Goodman, K. (1967) 'Reading, a psycholinguistic guessing game', *Journal of the Reading Specialist*, 5.

Hart, B and Rizley, T. A. (2003) 'The early catastrophe: the 3 million word gap by age 3', *American Educator*, Spring. Cited in Ross, C., McKechnie, E. F and Rothbauer, P. M. (2006) *Reading Matters: What the Research Reveals about Reading, Libraries and the Community*. Westport, CA: Libraries Unlimited.

Hobson, P. (2002) *The Cradle of Thought*. London: Macmillan.

Hornsby, B. (1999) *Alpha to Omega*. London: Heinemann.

Inkpen, M. (2006) *Penguin Small*. London: Hodder.

Johnston, R. and Watson, J. *The Effects of Synthetic Phonics Teaching on Reading and Spelling: A Seven-year Longtitudinal Study*. Edinburgh: Scottish Executive Central Research Unit.

Lunzer, E. and Gardner, K. (1984) *Reading for Learning in the Sciences, Learning from the Written Word*. Edinburgh: Oliver and Boyd for the Schools Council.

Oxford Companion to the English Language (2005) Oxford: Oxford University Press.

Neale Analysis of Reading Ability, 2nd revised British edn. (2997)Windsor: NFER-Nelson.

Ofsted (2005) Office for Standards in Education, Inspection Number 266863.

Palmer, S. (2006) *Toxic Childhood*. London: Bloomsbury.

Palmer, S. and Bayley, R. (2004) *Foundations of Literacy*. Stafford: Network Educational Press.

Perera, K. M. (1989) *The Development of Prosodic Features in Children's Oral Reading*. Unpublished Ph.D. thesis, University of Manchester.

Pinker, S. (1999) *Words and Rules*. London: Weidenfeld & Nicolson.

Pirrie, J. (1994) *On Common Ground*. Godalming: WWF.

Rose, J. (2006) *Independent Review of the Teaching of Reading*. London: DfES.

Rosen, M. and Oxenbury, H. (2003) *We're Going on a Bear Hunt*. London: Aladdin.

Ross, C., McKechnie, E. F and Rothbauer, P. M. (2006) *Reading Matters: What the Research Reveals about Reading. Libraries and the Community*. Westport, CA: Libraries Unlimited.

Schatz. E. K. and Baldwin, R. S. (1986) 'Contextual clues are unreliable predictors of word meanings', *Reading Research Quarterly*, 21.

Seuss, Dr (2007/1957) *The Cat in the Hat*. London: HarperCollins.

Shaughnessy, M. (ed.) (1977) *Errors and Expectations: A Guide for the Teacher of Basic Writing*. New York: Oxford University Press.

Smith, F. (1978) *Psycholinguistics and Reading*. New York: Holt, Reinhart and Winston.

Smith, F. (1978) *Reading*. Cambridge: Cambridge University Press.

Smith, F. (1994) *Understanding Reading*, 6th edn. New York: Erlbaum.

Snowling, M. and Stackhouse, J. (eds) (2005) *Dyslexia, Speech and Language*. Chichester: Wiley.

Tizard, B. and Hughes, M. (1984) *Young Children Learning*. London: Fontana.

Vygotsky, L. S. (1986) *Thought and Language*. Boston: MIT.

Vygotsky, L. S. (1987) *Mind in Society*. Cambridge, MA: Harvard University Press.

Ward, S. (1994) 'The validation of a treatment method for language delay in infants under one year of age'. Talk delivered at the CPLOL conference, Antwerp, 1994.

Wells, G. (1987) *The Meaning Makers*. London: Hodder & Stoughton.

Wilkins, A. (1995) *Visual Stress*. Oxford: Oxford University Press.

Wilkins, A. (2003) *Reading through Colour*. Chichester: Wiley.

Wragg, E. C. and Brown, G. (2001) *Explaining in the Primary School*. Abingdon: RoutledgeFalmer.

INDEX

Dedicated to the activists

the grassroots organisations,

th   challenge

the m   pecially to

T ony   Polaris

Institu   eard

                     sonally."

Also   Ralph   se of the

po:

Roddick

Proceeds from this book are going towards supporting visionaries, grassroots groups, and non-governmental organizations who are debunking the myths created by the World Trade Organization.

If you would like to re-use or reproduce any part of the text of this work then go ahead – email me for permission on book_duplicates@the-body-shop.com and I'll send you the copy. In return I ask that you use it well, credit the authors of any material you use, donate what you feel to be a fair sum to an appropriate NGO, and above all...

...Take It Personally

Thorsons
An Imprint of HarperCollinsPublishers
77–85 Fulham Palace Road,
Hammersmith, London W6 8JB

www.thorsons.com

Published by Thorsons 2001
10 9 8 7 6 5 4 3 2 1

Copyright © HarperCollins Publishers Ltd. 2001

Anita Roddick asserts the moral right to be identified as the author of this work

Publishing Director: Belinda Budge

Editor: Gavin Lewis

Design: Wheelhouse Creative Ltd.
www.wheelhousecreative.co.uk

Picture Research: Carolyn Watts

A catalogue record for this book is available from the British Library

ISBN 0 0071 2898 3

Printed in Great Britain by
The Bath Press, Bath

Printed on recycled paper